NATURE, ADDRESSES, AND LECTURES

BY

RALPH WALDO EMERSON

New and Revised Edition

BOSTON
HOUGHTON, MIFFLIN AND COMPANY
New York: 11 East Seventeenth Street
The Riverside Press, Cambridge

PS
1620
A1
1883

The Riverside Press, Cambridge, Mass., U. S. A.
Electrotyped and Printed by H. O. Houghton & Company.

PREFATORY NOTE.

THE first eight volumes of the present edition of Mr. Emerson's writings contain his collected Essays as he left them, except some revision of the punctuation and the correction of obvious mistakes. The ninth volume comprises the pieces chosen by Mr. Emerson from the "Poems" and "May-Day" to form the "Selected Poems," with the addition of some poems which were omitted in that selection, and some that have remained unpublished. In many instances emendations which were pencilled in the margin by Mr. Emerson, but were not adopted in the "Selected Poems," are now introduced, upon the ground that, as they seem to have suggested themselves at the time when his powers were in their fullest vigor, it may fairly be supposed that he would, upon reconsideration, have admitted them. The tenth and eleventh volumes consist of lectures hitherto unprinted, and of "Occasional Addresses" and other prose-writings which have appeared separately or in periodicals.

The selection from Mr. Emerson's MSS. has

been made in pursuance of the authority given in his will to me, as his literary executor, acting in co-operation with his children, to publish or withhold from publication any of his unpublished papers.

The portrait in the first volume was etched by Mr. Schoff from a photographic copy (kindly furnished by Mr. Alexander Ireland, of Manchester, England) of a daguerreotype taken in 1847 or 1848, probably in England.

J. E. CABOT.

CONTENTS.

———◆———

NATURE.

A SUBTLE chain of countless rings
The next unto the farthest brings ;
The eye reads omens where it goes,
And speaks all languages the rose ;
And, striving to be man, the worm
Mounts through all the spires of form.

INTRODUCTION.

———◆———

OUR age is retrospective. It builds the sepul-
chres of the fathers. It writes biographies, histories, and criticism. The foregoing generations
beheld God and nature face to face ; **we,** through
their eyes. Why should not we also enjoy an
original relation to the universe ? Why should
not we have a poetry and philosophy of insight
and not of tradition, and a religion by revelation
to us, and not the history of theirs ? Embosomed
for a season in nature, whose floods of life stream
around and through us, and invite us by the powers they supply, to action proportioned to nature,
why should we grope among the dry bones of the
past, or put the living generation into masquerade
out of its faded wardrobe ? The sun shines to-day
also. There is more wool and flax in the fields.
There are new lands, new men, new thoughts.
Let us demand our own works and laws and worship.

Undoubtedly we have no questions to ask which
are unanswerable. We must trust the perfection

of the creation so far as to believe that whatever curiosity the order of things has awakened in our minds, the order of things can satisfy. Every man's condition is a solution in hieroglyphic to those inquiries he would put. He acts it as life, before he apprehends it as truth. In like manner, nature is already, in its forms and tendencies, describing its own design. Let us interrogate the great apparition that shines so peacefully around us. Let us inquire, to what end is nature?

All science has one aim, namely, to find a theory of nature. We have theories of races and of functions, but scarcely yet a remote approach to an idea of creation. We are now so far from the road to truth, that religious teachers dispute and hate each other, and speculative men are esteemed unsound and frivolous. But to a sound judgment, the most abstract truth is the most practical. Whenever a true theory appears, it will be its own evidence. Its test is, that it will explain all phenomena. Now many are thought not only unexplained but inexplicable; as language, sleep, madness, dreams, beasts, sex.

Philosophically considered, the universe is composed of Nature and the Soul. Strictly speaking, therefore, all that is separate from us, all which Philosophy distinguishes as the NOT ME, that is, both nature and art, all other men and my own body, must be ranked under this name, NATURE. In enumerating the values of nature and casting up their sum, I shall use the word in both senses ; — in its common and in its philosophical import. In inquiries so general as our present one, the inaccuracy is not material ; no confusion of thought will occur. *Nature*, in the common sense, refers to essences unchanged by man ; space, the air, the river, the leaf. *Art* is applied to the mixture of his will with the same things, as in a house, a canal, a statue, a picture. But his operations taken together are so insignificant, a little chipping, baking, patching, and washing, that in an impression so grand as that of the world on the human mind, they do not vary the result.

NATURE.

———◆———

CHAPTER I.

To go into solitude, a man needs to retire as much from his chamber as from society. I am not solitary whilst I read and write, though nobody is with me. But if a man would be alone, let him look at the stars. The rays that come from those heavenly worlds will separate between him and what he touches. One might think the atmosphere was made transparent with this design, to give man, in the heavenly bodies, the perpetual presence of the sublime. Seen in the streets of cities, how great they are! If the stars should appear one night in a thousand years, how would men believe and adore; and preserve for many generations the remembrance of the city of God which had been shown! But every night come out these envoys of beauty, and light the universe with their admonishing smile.

The stars awaken a certain reverence, because though always present, they are inaccessible; but all natural objects make a kindred impression, when the mind is open to their influence. Nature never wears a mean appearance. Neither does the wisest man extort her secret, and lose his curiosity by finding out all her perfection. Nature never became a toy to a wise spirit. The flowers, the animals, the mountains, reflected the wisdom of his best hour, as much as they had delighted the simplicity of his childhood.

When we speak of nature in this manner, we have a distinct but most poetical sense in the mind. We mean the integrity of impression made by manifold natural objects. It is this which distinguishes the stick of timber of the wood-cutter, from the tree of the poet. The charming landscape which I saw this morning is indubitably made up of some twenty or thirty farms. Miller owns this field, Locke that, and Manning the woodland beyond. But none of them owns the landscape. There is a property in the horizon which no man has but he whose eye can integrate all the parts, that is, the poet. This is the best part of these men's farms, yet to this their warranty-deeds give no title.

To speak truly, few adult persons can see nature. Most persons do not see the sun. At least they have a very superficial seeing. The sun illuminates only the eye of the man, but shines into the eye and the heart of the child. The lover of nature is he whose inward and outward senses are still truly adjusted to each other; who has retained the spirit of infancy even into the era of manhood. His intercourse with heaven and earth becomes part of his daily food. In the presence of nature a wild delight runs through the man, in spite of real sorrows. Nature says, — he is my creature, and maugre all his impertinent griefs, he shall be glad with me. Not the sun or the summer alone, but every hour and season yields its tribute of delight; for every hour and change corresponds to and authorizes a different state of the mind, from breathless noon to grimmest midnight. Nature is a setting that fits equally well a comic or a mourning piece. In good health, the air is a cordial of incredible virtue. Crossing a bare common, in snow puddles, at twilight, under a clouded sky, without having in my thoughts any occurrence of special good fortune, I have enjoyed a perfect exhilaration. I am glad to the brink of fear. In the woods, too, a man casts off his years, as the snake his slough, and at what period soever of life, is always a child. In the woods is perpetual youth. Within these plantations of God, a decorum and sanctity reign, a perennial festival is dressed, and the guest sees not how he should tire of them in a thousand years. In the woods, we return to reason and faith. There I feel that nothing can befall me in life, — no disgrace, no calamity (leaving me my eyes), which nature cannot repair. Standing on the bare ground,

— my head bathed by the blithe air, and uplifted into infinite space, — all mean egotism vanishes. I become a transparent eye-ball; I am nothing; I see all; the currents of the Universal Being circulate through me; I am part or parcel of God. The name of the nearest friend sounds then foreign and accidental: to be brothers, to be acquaintances, — master or servant, is then a trifle and a disturbance. I am the lover of uncontained and immortal beauty. In the wilderness, I find something more dear and connate than in streets or villages. In the tranquil landscape, and especially in the distant line of the horizon, man beholds somewhat as beautiful as his own nature.

The greatest delight which the fields and woods minister is the suggestion of an occult relation between man and the vegetable. I am not alone and unacknowledged. They nod to me, and I to them. The waving of the boughs in the storm is new to me and old. It takes me by surprise, and yet is not unknown. Its effect is like that of a higher thought or a better emotion coming over me, when I deemed I was thinking justly or doing right.

Yet it is certain that the power to produce this delight does not reside in nature, but in man, or in a harmony of both. It is necessary to use these pleasures with great temperance. For nature is not always tricked in holiday attire, but the same scene which yesterday breathed perfume and glittered as for the frolic of the nymphs, is overspread with melancholy to-day. Nature always wears the colors of the spirit. To a man laboring under calamity, the heat of his own fire hath sadness in it. Then there is a kind of contempt of the landscape felt by him who has just lost by death a dear friend. The sky is less grand as it shuts down over less worth in the population.

CHAPTER II.

COMMODITY.

WHOEVER considers the final cause of the world will discern a multitude of uses that enter as parts into that result. They all admit of being thrown into one of the following classes: Commodity; Beauty; Language; and Discipline.

Under the general name of commodity, I rank all those advantages which our senses owe to nature. This, of course, is a benefit which is temporary and mediate, not ultimate, like its service to the soul. Yet although low, it is perfect in its kind, and is the only use of nature which all men apprehend. The misery of man appears like childish petulance, when we explore the steady and prodigal provision that has been made for his support and delight on this green ball which floats him through the heavens. What angels invented these splendid ornaments, these rich conveniences, this ocean of air above, this ocean of water beneath, this firmament of earth between? this zodiac of lights, this tent of dropping clouds, this striped coat of climates, this fourfold year? Beasts, fire, water, stones, and corn serve him. The field is at once his floor, his work-yard, his play-ground, his garden, and his bed.

> " More servants wait on man
> Than he 'll take notice of."

Nature, in its ministry to man, is not only the material, but is also the process and the result. All the parts incessantly work into each other's hands for the profit of man. The wind sows the seed ; the sun evaporates the sea; the wind blows the vapor to the field ; the ice, on the other side of the planet, condenses rain on this; the rain feeds the plant ; the plant feeds the animal ; and thus the endless circulations of the divine charity nourish man.

The useful arts are reproductions or new combinations by the wit of man, of the same natural benefactors. He no longer waits for favoring gales, but by means of steam, he realizes the fable of Æolus's bag, and carries the two and thirty winds in the boiler of his boat. To diminish friction, he paves the road with iron bars, and, mounting a coach with a ship-load of men, animals, and merchandise behind him, he darts through the country, from town to town, like an eagle or a swallow through the air. By the aggregate of these aids, how is the face of the world changed, from the era of Noah to that of Napoleon ! The private poor man hath cities, ships, canals, bridges, built for him. He goes to the post-office, and the human race run on his errands; to the book-shop, and the human race read and write of all that happens, for him; to the court-house, and nations repair his wrongs. He sets his house upon the road, and the human race go forth every morning, and shovel out the snow, and cut a path for him.

But there is no need of specifying particulars in this class of uses. The catalogue is endless, and the examples so obvious, that I shall leave them to the reader's reflection, with the general remark, that this mercenary benefit is one which has respect to a farther good. A man is fed, not that he may be fed, but that he may work.

CHAPTER III.

A NOBLER want of man is served by nature, namely, the love of Beauty.

The ancient Greeks called the world κόσμος, beauty. Such is the constitution of all things, or such the plastic power of the human eye, that the primary forms, as the sky, the mountain, the tree, the animal, give us a delight *in and for themselves;* a pleasure arising from outline, color, motion, and grouping. This seems partly owing to the eye itself. The eye is the best of artists. By the mutual action of its structure and of the laws of light, perspective is produced, which integrates every mass of objects, of what character soever, into a well colored and shaded globe, so that where the particular objects are mean and unaffecting, the landscape which they compose is round and symmetrical. And as the eye is the best composer, so light is the first of painters. There is no object so foul that intense light will not make beautiful. And the stimulus it affords to the sense, and a sort of infinitude which it hath, like space and

time, make all matter gay. Even the corpse has
its own beauty. But besides this general grace
diffused over nature, almost all the individual
forms are agreeable to the eye, as is proved by
our endless imitations of some of them, as the
acorn, the grape, the pine-cone, the wheat-ear, the
egg, the wings and forms of most birds, the lion's
claw, the serpent, the butterfly, sea-shells, flames,
clouds, buds, leaves, and the forms of many trees,
as the palm.

For better consideration, we may distribute the
aspects of Beauty in a threefold manner.

1. First, the simple perception of natural forms
is a delight. The influence of the forms and actions in nature is so needful to man, that, in its
lowest functions, it seems to lie on the confines of
commodity and beauty. To the body and mind
which have been cramped by noxious work or
company, nature is medicinal and restores their
tone. The tradesman, the attorney comes out of
the din and craft of the street and sees the sky
and the woods, and is a man again. In their eternal calm, he finds himself. The health of the eye
seems to demand a horizon. We are never tired,
so long as we can see far enough.

But in other hours, Nature satisfies by its loveliness, and without any mixture of corporeal benefit.
I see the spectacle of morning from the hill-top

over against my house, from day-break to sun-rise, with emotions which an angel might share. The long slender bars of cloud float like fishes in the sea of crimson light. From the earth, as a shore, I look out into that silent sea. I seem to partake its rapid transformations; the active enchantment reaches my dust, and I dilate and conspire with the morning wind. How does Nature deify us with a few and cheap elements! Give me health and a day, and I will make the pomp of emperors ridiculous. The dawn is my Assyria; the sunset and moon-rise my Paphos, and unimaginable realms of faerie; broad noon shall be my England of the senses and the understanding; the night shall be my Germany of mystic philosophy and dreams.

Not less excellent, except for our less susceptibility in the afternoon, was the charm, last evening, of a January sunset. The western clouds divided and subdivided themselves into pink flakes modulated with tints of unspeakable softness, and the air had so much life and sweetness that it was a pain to come within doors. What was it that nature would say? Was there no meaning in the live repose of the valley behind the mill, and which Homer or Shakspeare could not re-form for me in words? The leafless trees become spires of flame in the sunset, with the blue east for their back-

ground, and the stars of the dead calices of flowers, and every withered stem and stubble rimed
with frost, contribute something to the mute music.

The inhabitants of cities suppose that the country landscape is pleasant only half the year. I
please myself with the graces of the winter scenery, and believe that we are as much touched by it
as by the genial influences of summer. To the at-
tentive eye, each moment of the year has its own
beauty, and in the same field, it beholds, every
hour, a picture which was never seen before, and
which shall never be seen again. The heavens
change every moment, and reflect their glory or
gloom on the plains beneath. The state of the
crop in the surrounding farms alters the expression
of the earth from week to week. The succession
of native plants in the pastures and roadsides,
which makes the silent clock by which time tells
the summer hours, will make even the divisions of
the day sensible to a keen observer. The tribes of
birds and insects, like the plants punctual to their
time, follow each other, and the year has room for
all. By watercourses, the variety is greater. In
July, the blue pontederia or pickerel-weed blooms
in large beds in the shallow parts of our pleasant
river, and swarms with yellow butterflies in continual motion. Art cannot rival this pomp of pur-

ple and gold. Indeed the river is a perpetual gala, and boasts each month a new ornament.

But this beauty of Nature which is seen and felt as beauty, is the least part. The shows of day, the dewy morning, the rainbow, mountains, orchards in blossom, stars, moonlight, shadows in still water, and the like, if too eagerly hunted, become shows merely, and mock us with their unreality. Go out of the house to see the moon, and 't is mere tinsel; it will not please as when its light shines upon your necessary journey. The beauty that shimmers in the yellow afternoons of October, who ever could clutch it? Go forth to find it, and it is gone; 't is only a mirage as you look from the windows of diligence.

2. The presence of a higher, namely, of the spiritual element is essential to its perfection. The high and divine beauty which can be loved without effeminacy, is that which is found in combination with the human will. Beauty is the mark God sets upon virtue. Every natural action is graceful. Every heroic act is also decent, and causes the place and the bystanders to shine. We are taught by great actions that the universe is the property of every individual in it. Every rational creature has all nature for his dowry and estate. It is his, if he will. He may divest himself of it; he may creep into a corner, and abdicate his kingdom, as

most men do, but he is entitled to the world by his constitution. In proportion to the energy of his thought and will, he takes up the world into himself. " All those things for which men plough, build, or sail, obey virtue ; " said Sallust. " The winds and waves," said Gibbon, " are always on the side of the ablest navigators." So are the sun and moon and all the stars of heaven. When a noble act is done, — perchance in a scene of great natural beauty ; when Leonidas and his three hundred martyrs consume one day in dying, and the sun and moon come each and look at them once in the steep defile of Thermopylæ ; when Arnold Winkelried, in the high Alps, under the shadow of the avalanche, gathers in his side a sheaf of Austrian spears to break the line for his comrades ; are not these heroes entitled to add the beauty of the scene to the beauty of the deed ? When the bark of Columbus nears the shore of America ; — before it, the beach lined with savages, fleeing out of all their huts of cane ; the sea behind ; and the purple mountains of the Indian Archipelago around, can we separate the man from the living picture ? Does not the New World clothe his form with her palm-groves and savannahs as fit drapery ? Ever does natural beauty steal in like air, and envelope great actions. When Sir Harry Vane was dragged up the Tower-hill, sitting on a sled, to suffer death as the champion of the English laws, one of the multitude cried out to him, "You never sate on so glorious a seat!" Charles II., to intimidate the citizens of London, caused the patriot Lord Russell to be drawn in an open coach through the principal streets of the city on his way to the scaffold. "But," his biographer says, "the multitude imagined they saw liberty and virtue sitting by his side." In private places, among sordid objects, an act of truth or heroism seems at once to draw to itself the sky as its temple, the sun as its candle. Nature stretches out her arms to embrace man, only let his thoughts be of equal greatness. Willingly does she follow his steps with the rose and the violet, and bend her lines of grandeur and grace to the decoration of her darling child. Only let his thoughts be of equal scope, and the frame will suit the picture. A virtuous man is in unison with her works, and makes the central figure of the visible sphere. Homer, Pindar, Socrates, Phocion, associate themselves fitly in our memory with the geography and climate of Greece. The visible heavens and earth sympathize with Jesus. And in common life whosoever has seen a person of powerful character and happy genius, will have remarked how easily he took all things along with him, — the persons, the opinions, and the day, and nature became ancillary to a man.

3. There is still another aspect under which the beauty of the world may be viewed, namely, as it becomes an object of the intellect. Beside the relation of things to virtue, they have a relation to thought. The intellect searches out the absolute order of things as they stand in the mind of God, and without the colors of affection. The intellectual and the active powers seem to succeed each other, and the exclusive activity of the one generates the exclusive activity of the other. There is something unfriendly in each to the other, but they are like the alternate periods of feeding and working in animals; each prepares and will be followed by the other. Therefore does beauty, which, in relation to actions, as we have seen, comes unsought, and comes because it is unsought, remain for the apprehension and pursuit of the intellect; and then again, in its turn, of the active power. Nothing divine dies. All good is eternally reproductive. The beauty of nature re-forms itself in the mind, and not for barren contemplation, but for new creation.

All men are in some degree impressed by the face of the world; some men even to delight. This love of beauty is Taste. Others have the same love in such excess, that, not content with admiring, they seek to embody it in new forms. The creation of beauty is Art.

The production of a work of art throws a light upon the mystery of humanity. A work of art is an abstract or epitome of the world. It is the result or expression of nature, in miniature. For although the works of nature are innumerable and all different, the result or the expression of them all is similar and single. Nature is a sea of forms radically alike and even unique. A leaf, a sunbeam, a landscape, the ocean, make an analogous impression on the mind. What is common to them all, — that perfectness and harmony, is beauty. The standard of beauty is the entire circuit of natural forms, — the totality of nature; which the Italians expressed by defining beauty "il piu nell' uno." Nothing is quite beautiful alone; nothing but is beautiful in the whole. A single object is only so far beautiful as it suggests this universal grace. The poet, the painter, the sculptor, the musician, the architect, seek each to concentrate this radiance of the world on one point, and each in his several work to satisfy the love of beauty which stimulates him to produce. Thus is Art a nature passed through the alembic of man. Thus in art does Nature work through the will of a man filled with the beauty of her first works.

The world thus exists to the soul to satisfy the desire of beauty. This element I call an ultimate end. No reason can be asked or given why the

soul seeks beauty. Beauty, in its largest and profoundest sense, is one expression for the universe.
God is the all-fair. Truth, and goodness, and
beauty, are but different faces of the same All.
But beauty in nature is not ultimate. It is the
herald of inward and eternal beauty, and is not
alone a solid and satisfactory good. It must stand
as a part, and not as yet the last or highest expression of the final cause of Nature.

CHAPTER IV.

LANGUAGE.

LANGUAGE is a third use which Nature subserves to man. Nature is the vehicle of thought, and in a simple, double, and three-fold degree.

1. Words are signs of natural facts.

2. Particular natural facts are symbols of particular spiritual facts.

3. Nature is the symbol of spirit.

1. Words are signs of natural facts. The use of natural history is to give us aid in supernatural history; the use of the outer creation, to give us language for the beings and changes of the inward creation. Every word which is used to express a moral or intellectual fact, if traced to its root, is found to be borrowed from some material appearance. *Right* means *straight; wrong* means *twisted.* *Spirit* primarily means *wind; transgression*, the crossing of a *line; supercilious*, the *raising of the eyebrow*. We say the *heart* to express emotion, the *head* to denote thought; and *thought* and *emotion* are words borrowed from sensible things, and now appropriated to spiritual

nature. Most of the process by which this trans-
formation is made, is hidden from us in the remote time when language was framed; but the
same tendency may be daily observed in children.
Children and savages use only nouns or names of
things, which they convert into verbs, and apply to
analogous mental acts.

2. But this origin of all words that convey a
spiritual import, — so conspicuous a fact in the history of language, — is our least debt to nature. It
is not words only that are emblematic; it is things
which are emblematic. Every natural fact is a
symbol of some spiritual fact. Every appearance
in nature corresponds to some state of the mind,
and that state of the mind can only be described
by presenting that natural appearance as its picture. An enraged man is a lion, a cunning man is
a fox, a firm man is a rock, a learned man is a
torch. A lamb is innocence; a snake is subtle
spite; flowers express to us the delicate affections.
Light and darkness are our familiar expression for
knowledge and ignorance; and heat for love. Visible distance behind and before us, is respectively
our image of memory and hope.

Who looks upon a river in a meditative hour
and is not reminded of the flux of all things?
Throw a stone into the stream, and the circles that
propagate themselves are the beautiful type of all

influence.   Man is conscious of a universal soul
within or behind his individual life, wherein, as in
a firmament, the natures of Justice, Truth, Love,
Freedom, arise and shine.   This universal soul
he calls Reason : it is not mine, or thine, or his,
but we are its ; we are its property and men.   And
the blue sky in which the private earth is buried,
the sky with its eternal calm, and full of everlasting orbs, is the type of Reason.   That which intellectually considered we call Reason, considered in
relation to nature, we call Spirit.   Spirit is the
Creator.   Spirit hath life in itself.   And man in
all ages and countries embodies it in his language
as the FATHER.

It is easily seen that there is nothing lucky or
capricious in these analogies, but that they are
constant, and pervade nature.   These are not the
dreams of a few poets, here and there, but man is
an analogist, and studies relations in all objects.
He is placed in the centre of beings, and a ray of
relation passes from every other being to him.
And neither can man be understood without these
objects, nor these objects without man.   All the
facts in natural history taken by themselves, have
no value, but are barren, like a single sex.   But
marry it to human history, and it is full of life.
Whole floras, all Linnæus' and Buffon's volumes,
are dry catalogues of facts ; but the most trivial of

these facts, the habit of a plant, the organs, or
work, or noise of an insect, applied to the illustration of a fact in intellectual philosophy, or in any
way associated to human nature, affects us in the
most lively and agreeable manner. The seed of a
plant, — to what affecting analogies in the nature
of man is that little fruit made use of, in all discourse, up to the voice of Paul, who calls the human corpse a seed, — "It is sown a natural body;
it is raised a spiritual body." The motion of the
earth round its axis and round the sun, makes the
day and the year. These are certain amounts of
brute light and heat. But is there no intent of an
analogy between man's life and the seasons? And
do the seasons gain no grandeur or pathos from
that analogy? The instincts of the ant are very
unimportant considered as the ant's; but the moment a ray of relation is seen to extend from it to
man, and the little drudge is seen to be a monitor,
a little body with a mighty heart, then all its habits, even that said to be recently observed, that it
never sleeps, become sublime.

Because of this radical correspondence between
visible things and human thoughts, savages, who
have only what is necessary, converse in figures.
As we go back in history, language becomes more
picturesque, until its infancy, when it is all poetry;
or all spiritual facts are represented by natural

symbols. The same symbols are found to make
the original elements of all languages. It has
moreover been observed, that the idioms of all
languages approach each other in passages of the
greatest eloquence and power. And as this is the
first language, so is it the last. This immediate
dependence of language upon nature, this conversion of an outward phenomenon into a type of
somewhat in human life, never loses its power to
affect us. It is this which gives that piquancy to
the conversation of a strong-natured farmer or
backwoodsman, which all men relish.

A man's power to connect his thought with its
proper symbol, and so to utter it, depends on the
simplicity of his character, that is, upon his love
of truth and his desire to communicate it without
loss. The corruption of man is followed by the corruption of language. When simplicity of character
and the sovereignty of ideas is broken up by the
prevalence of secondary desires, the desire of riches,
of pleasure, of power, and of praise, — and duplic-
ity and falsehood take place of simplicity and truth,
the power over nature as an interpreter of the will
is in a degree lost; new imagery ceases to be created, and old words are perverted to stand for things
which are not; a paper currency is employed, when
there is no bullion in the vaults. In due time the
fraud is manifest, and words lose all power to stim-

ulate the understanding or the affections. Hundreds of writers may be found in every long-civilized nation who for a short time believe and make others believe that they see and utter truths, who do not of themselves clothe one thought in its natural garment, but who feed unconsciously on the language created by the primary writers of the country, those, namely, who hold primarily on nature.

But wise men pierce this rotten diction and fasten words again to visible things; so that picturesque language is at once a commanding certificate that he who employs it is a man in alliance with truth and God. The moment our discourse rises above the ground line of familiar facts and is inflamed with passion or exalted by thought, it clothes itself in images. A man conversing in earnest, if he watch his intellectual processes, will find that a material image more or less luminous arises in his mind, contemporaneous with every thought, which furnishes the vestment of the thought. Hence, good writing and brilliant discourse are perpetual allegories. This imagery is spontaneous. It is the blending of experience with the present action of the mind. It is proper creation. It is the working of the Original Cause through the instruments he has already made.

These facts may suggest the advantage which the country-life possesses, for a powerful mind, over the artificial and curtailed life of cities. We know more from nature than we can at will communicate. Its light flows into the mind evermore, and we forget its presence. The poet, the orator, bred in the woods, whose senses have been nourished by their fair and appeasing changes, year after year, without design and without heed, — shall not lose their lesson altogether, in the roar of cities or the broil of politics. Long hereafter, amidst agitation and terror in national councils, — in the hour of revolution, — these solemn images shall reappear in their morning lustre, as fit symbols and words of the thoughts which the passing events shall awaken. At the call of a noble sentiment, again the woods wave, the pines murmur, the river rolls and shines, and the cattle low upon the mountains, as he saw and heard them in his infancy. And with these forms, the spells of persuasion, the keys of power are put into his hands.

3. We are thus assisted by natural objects in the expression of particular meanings. But how great a language to convey such pepper-corn informations! Did it need such noble races of creatures, this profusion of forms, this host of orbs in heaven, to furnish man with the dictionary and grammar of his municipal speech? Whilst we use this grand cipher to expedite the affairs of our pot and kettle, we feel that we have not yet put it to its use, neither are

able.   We are like travellers using the cinders of
a volcano to roast their eggs.   Whilst we see that
it always stands ready to clothe what we would say,
we cannot avoid the question whether the characters are not significant of themselves.   Have mountains, and waves, and skies, no significance but what
we consciously give them when we employ them as
emblems of our thoughts?   The world is emblematic.   Parts of speech are metaphors, because the
whole of nature is a metaphor of the human mind.
The laws of moral nature answer to those of matter as face to face in a glass.   "The visible world
and the relation of its parts, is the dial plate of the
invisible."   The axioms of physics translate the
laws of ethics.   Thus, "the whole is greater than its
part;" "reaction is equal to action;" "the smallest weight may be made to lift the greatest, the difference of weight being compensated by time;" and
many the like propositions, which have an ethical as
well as physical sense.   These propositions have a
much more extensive and universal sense when applied to human life, than when confined to techni-
cal use.

In like manner, the memorable words of history
and the proverbs of nations consist usually of a
natural fact, selected as a picture or parable of a
moral truth.   Thus; A rolling stone gathers no
moss; A bird in the hand is worth two in the bush;

A cripple in the right way will beat a racer in the wrong; Make hay while the sun shines; 'T is hard to carry a full cup even; Vinegar is the son of wine; The last ounce broke the camel's back; Long-lived trees make roots first; — and the like. In their primary sense these are trivial facts, but we repeat them for the value of their analogical import. What is true of proverbs, is true of all fables, parables, and allegories.

This relation between the mind and matter *is* not fancied by some poet, but stands in the will of God, and so is free to be known by all men. It appears to men, or it does not appear. When in fortunate hours we ponder this miracle, the wise man doubts if at all other times he is not blind and deaf;

> " Can these things be,
> And overcome us like a summer's cloud,
> Without our special wonder ? "

for the universe becomes transparent, and the light of higher laws than its own shines through it. It is the standing problem which has exercised the wonder and the study of every fine genius since the world began; from the era of the Egyptians and the Brahmins to that of Pythagoras, of Plato, of Bacon, of Leibnitz, of Swedenborg. There sits the Sphinx at the road-side, and from age to age, as each prophet comes by, he tries his fortune at reading her riddle. There seems to be a necessity in spirit to manifest itself in material forms; and day and night, river and storm, beast and bird, acid and alkali, preëxist in necessary Ideas in the mind of God, and are what they are by virtue of preceding affections in the world of spirit. A Fact is the end or last issue of spirit. The visible creation is the terminus or the circumference of the invisible world. " Material objects," said a French philosopher, " are necessarily kinds of *scoriæ* of the substantial thoughts of the Creator, which must always preserve an exact relation to their first origin; in other words, visible nature must have a spiritual and moral side."

This doctrine is abstruse, and though the images of "garment," "scoriæ," "mirror," &c., may stimulate the fancy, we must summon the aid of subtler and more vital expositors to make it plain. " Every scripture is to be interpreted by the same spirit which gave it forth," — is the fundamental law of criticism. A life in harmony with Nature, the love of truth and of virtue, will purge the eyes to understand her text. By degrees we may come to know the primitive sense of the permanent objects of nature, so that the world shall be to us an open book, and every form significant of its hidden life and final cause.

A new interest surprises us, whilst, under the

view now suggested, we contemplate the fearful extent and multitude of objects; since "every object rightly seen, unlocks a new faculty of the soul." That which was unconscious truth, becomes, when interpreted and defined in an object, a part of the domain of knowledge, — a new weapon in the magazine of power.

CHAPTER V.

DISCIPLINE.

IN view of the significance of nature, we arrive at once at a new fact, that nature is a discipline. This use of the world includes the preceding uses, as parts of itself.

Space, time, society, labor, climate, food, locomotion, the animals, the mechanical forces, give us sincerest lessons, day by day, whose meaning is unlimited. They educate both the Understanding and the Reason. Every property of matter is a school for the understanding, — its solidity or resistance, its inertia, its extension, its figure, its divisibility. The understanding adds, divides, combines, measures, and finds nutriment and room for its activity in this worthy scene. Meantime, Reason transfers all these lessons into its own world of thought, by perceiving the analogy that marries Matter and Mind.

1. Nature is a discipline of the understanding in intellectual truths. Our dealing with sensible objects is a constant exercise in the necessary lessons of difference, of likeness, of order, of being and

seeming, of progressive arrangement; of ascent from particular to general ; of combination to one end of manifold forces. Proportioned to the importance of the organ to be formed, is the extreme care with which its tuition is provided, — a care pretermitted in no single case. What tedious training, day after day, year after year, never ending, to form the common sense ; what continual reproduction of annoyances, inconveniences, dilemmas ; what rejoicing over us of little men ; what disputing of prices, what reckonings of interest, — and all to form the Hand of the mind ; — to instruct us that " good thoughts are no better than good dreams, unless they be executed ! "

The same good office is performed by Property and its filial systems of debt and credit. Debt, grinding debt, whose iron face the widow, the orphan, and the sons of genius fear and hate ; — debt, which consumes so much time, which so cripples and disheartens a great spirit with cares that seem so base, is a preceptor whose lessons cannot be forgone, and is needed most by those who suffer from it most. Moreover, property, which has been well compared to snow, — " if it fall level today, it will be blown into drifts to-morrow," — is the surface action of internal machinery, like the index on the face of a clock. Whilst now it is the gymnastics of the understanding, it is hiving, in the foresight of the spirit, experience in profounder laws.

The whole character and fortune of the individual are affected by the least inequalities in the culture of the understanding; for example, in the perception of differences. Therefore is Space, and therefore Time, that man may know that things are not huddled and lumped, but sundered and individual. A bell and a plough have each their use, and neither can do the office of the other. Water is good to drink, coal to burn, wool to wear; but wool cannot be drunk, nor water spun, nor coal eaten. The wise man shows his wisdom in separation, in gradation, and his scale of creatures and of merits is as wide as nature. The foolish have no range in their scale, but suppose every man is as every other man. What is not good they call the worst, and what is not hateful, they call the best.

In like manner, what good heed Nature forms in us! She pardons no mistakes. Her yea is yea, and her nay, nay.

The first steps in Agriculture, Astronomy, Zoology (those first steps which the farmer, the hunter, and the sailor take), teach that Nature's dice are always loaded; that in her heaps and rubbish are concealed sure and useful results.

How calmly and genially the mind apprehends one after another the laws of physics! What noble emotions dilate the mortal as he enters into the counsels of the creation, and feels by knowledge the privilege to BE! His insight refines him. The beauty of nature shines in his own breast. Man is greater that he can see this, and the universe less, because Time and Space relations vanish as laws are known.

Here again we are impressed and even daunted by the immense Universe to be explored. " What we know is a point to what we do not know." Open any recent journal of science, and weigh the problems suggested concerning Light, Heat, Electricity, Magnetism, Physiology, Geology, and judge whether the interest of natural science is likely to be soon exhausted.

Passing by many particulars of the discipline of nature, we must not omit to specify two.

The exercise of the Will, or the lesson of power, is taught in every event. From the child's successive possession of his several senses up to the hour when he saith, " Thy will be done ! " he is learning the secret that he can reduce under his will, not only particular events but great classes, nay, the whole series of events, and so conform all facts to his character. Nature is thoroughly mediate. It is made to serve. It receives the dominion of man as meekly as the ass on which the Saviour rode. It offers all its kingdoms to man as the

raw material which he may mould into what is useful. Man is never weary of working it up. He
forges the subtile and delicate air into wise and
melodious words, and gives them wing as angels of
persuasion and command. One after another his
victorious thought comes up with and reduces all
things, until the world becomes at last only a realized will, — the double of the man.

2. Sensible objects conform to the premonitions
of Reason and reflect the conscience. All things
are moral; and in their boundless changes have an
unceasing reference to spiritual nature. Therefore
is nature glorious with form, color, and motion;
that every globe in the remotest heaven, every
chemical change from the rudest crystal up to the
laws of life, every change of vegetation from the
first principle of growth in the eye of a leaf, to the
tropical forest and antediluvian coal-mine, every
animal function from the sponge up to Hercules,
shall hint or thunder to man the laws of right and
wrong, and echo the Ten Commandments. Therefore is Nature ever the ally of Religion : lends all
her pomp and riches to the religious sentiment.
Prophet and priest, David, Isaiah, Jesus, have
drawn deeply from this source. This ethical character so penetrates the bone and marrow of nature,
as to seem the end for which it was made. Whatever private purpose is answered by any member

or part, this is its public and universal function, and is never omitted. Nothing in nature is exhausted in its first use. When a thing has served an end to the uttermost, it is wholly new for an ulterior service. In God, every end is converted into a new means. Thus the use of commodity, regarded by itself, is mean and squalid. But it is to the mind an education in the doctrine of Use, namely, that a thing is good only so far as it serves; that a conspiring of parts and efforts to the production of an end is essential to any being. The first and gross manifestation of this truth is our inevitable and hated training in values and wants, in corn and meat.

It has already been illustrated, that every natural process is a version of a moral sentence. The moral law lies at the centre of nature and radiates to the circumference. It is the pith and marrow of every substance, every relation, and every process. All things with which we deal, preach to us. What is a farm but a mute gospel? The chaff and the wheat, weeds and plants, blight, rain, insects, sun, — it is a sacred emblem from the first furrow of spring to the last stack which the snow of winter overtakes in the fields. But the sailor, the shepherd, the miner, the merchant, in their several resorts, have each an experience precisely parallel, and leading to the same conclusion: because all organizations are radically alike. Nor can it be doubted that this moral sentiment which thus scents the air, grows in the grain, and impregnates the waters of the world, is caught by man and sinks into his soul. The moral influence of nature upon every individual is that amount of truth which it illustrates to him. Who can estimate this? Who can guess how much firmness the sea-beaten rock has taught the fisherman? how much tranquillity has been reflected to man from the azure sky, over whose unspotted deeps the winds forevermore drive flocks of stormy clouds, and leave no wrinkle or stain? how much industry and providence and affection we have caught from the pantomime of brutes? What a searching preacher of self-command is the varying phenomenon of Health!

Herein is especially apprehended the unity of Nature, — the unity in variety, — which meets us everywhere. All the endless variety of things make an identical impression. Xenophanes complained in his old age, that, look where he would, all things hastened back to Unity. He was weary of seeing the same entity in the tedious variety of forms. The fable of Proteus has a cordial truth. A leaf, a drop, a crystal, a moment of time, is related to the whole, and partakes of the perfection of the whole. Each particle is a microcosm, and faithfully renders the likeness of the world.

Not only resemblances exist in things whose analogy is obvious, as when we detect the type of the human hand in the flipper of the fossil saurus, but also in objects wherein there is great superficial unlikeness. Thus architecture is called "frozen music," by De Staël and Goethe. Vitruvius thought an architect should be a musician. "A Gothic church," said Coleridge, "is a petrified religion." Michael Angelo maintained, that, to an architect, a knowledge of anatomy is essential. In Haydn's oratorios, the notes present to the imagination not only motions, as of the snake, the stag, and the elephant, but colors also; as the green grass. The law of harmonic sounds reappears in the harmonic colors. The granite is differenced in its laws only by the more or less of heat from the river that wears it away. The river, as it flows, resembles the air that flows over it; the air resembles the light which traverses it with more subtile currents; the light resembles the heat which rides with it through Space. Each creature is only a modification of the other; the likeness in them is more than the difference, and their radical law is one and the same. A rule of one art, or a law of one organization, holds true throughout nature. So intimate is this Unity, that, it is easily seen, it lies under the undermost garment of nature, and betrays its source in Universal Spirit. For it pervades Thought also. Every universal truth which we express in words, implies or supposes every other truth. *Omne verum vero consonat.* It is like a great circle on a sphere, comprising all possible circles ; which, however, may be drawn and comprise it in like manner. Every such truth is the absolute Ens seen from one side. But it has innumerable sides.

The central Unity is still more conspicuous in actions. Words are finite organs of the infinite mind. They cannot cover the dimensions of what is in truth. They break, chop, and impoverish it. An action is the perfection and publication of thought. A right action seems to fill the eye, and to be related to all nature. " The wise man, in doing one thing, does all ; or, in the one thing he does rightly, he sees the likeness of all which is done rightly."

Words and actions are not the attributes of brute nature. They introduce us to the human form, of which all other organizations appear to be degradations. When this appears among so many that surround it, the spirit prefers it to all others. It says, " From such as this have I drawn joy and knowledge ; in such as this have I found and beheld myself ; I will speak to it; it can speak again; it can yield me thought already formed and alive." In fact, the eye, — the mind, — is always accompanied by these forms, male and female; and these are incomparably the richest informations of the power and order that lie at the heart of things. Unfortunately every one of them bears the marks as of some injury; is marred and superficially defective. Nevertheless, far different from the deaf and dumb nature around them, these all rest like fountain-pipes on the unfathomed sea of thought and virtue whereto they alone, of all organizations, are the entrances.

It were a pleasant inquiry to follow into detail their ministry to our education, but where would it stop? We are associated in adolescent and adult life with some friends, who, like skies and waters, are coextensive with our idea; who, answering each to a certain affection of the soul, satisfy our desire on that side; whom we lack power to put at such focal distance from us, that we can mend or even analyze them. We cannot choose but love them. When much intercourse with a friend has supplied us with a standard of excellence, and has increased our respect for the resources of God who thus sends a real person to outgo our ideal; when he has, moreover, become an object of thought, and, whilst his character retains all its unconscious effect, is converted in the mind into solid and sweet wisdom, — it is a sign to us that his office is closing, and he is commonly withdrawn from our sight in a short time.

CHAPTER VI.

IDEALISM.

THUS is the unspeakable but intelligible and practicable meaning of the world conveyed to man, the immortal pupil, in every object of sense. To this one end of Discipline, all parts of nature conspire.

A noble doubt perpetually suggests itself, — whether this end be not the Final Cause of the Universe; and whether nature outwardly exists. It is a sufficient account of that Appearance we call the World, that God will teach a human mind, and so makes it the receiver of a certain number of congruent sensations, which we call sun and moon, man and woman, house and trade. In my utter impotence to test the authenticity of the report of my senses, to know whether the impressions they make on me correspond with outlying objects, what difference does it make, whether Orion is up there in heaven, or some god paints the image in the firmament of the soul? The relations of parts and the end of the whole remaining the same, what is the difference, whether land and sea inter-

act, and worlds revolve and intermingle without
number or end, — deep yawning under deep,
and galaxy balancing galaxy, throughout absolute
space, — or whether, without relations of time
and space, the same appearances are inscribed in
the constant faith of man? Whether nature enjoy a substantial existence without, or is only in
the apocalypse of the mind, it is alike useful and
alike venerable to me. Be it what it may, it is
ideal to me so long as I cannot try the accuracy of
my senses.

The frivolous make themselves merry with the
Ideal theory, as if its consequences were burlesque;
as if it affected the stability of nature. It surely
does not. God never jests with us, and will not
compromise the end of nature by permitting any
inconsequence in its procession. Any distrust of
the permanence of laws would paralyze the faculties of man. Their permanence is sacredly respected, and his faith therein is perfect. The
wheels and springs of man are all set to the hypothesis of the permanence of nature. We are not
built like a ship to be tossed, but like a house to
stand. It is a natural consequence of this structure, that so long as the active powers predominate
over the reflective, we resist with indignation any
hint that nature is more short-lived or mutable
than spirit. The broker, the wheelwright, the car-

penter, the tollman, are much displeased at the intimation.

But whilst we acquiesce entirely in the permanence of natural laws, the question of the absolute existence of nature still remains open. It is the uniform effect of culture on the human mind, not to shake our faith in the stability of particular phenomena, as of heat, water, azote; but to lead us to regard nature as phenomenon, not a substance; to attribute necessary existence to spirit; to esteem nature as an accident and an effect.

To the senses and the unrenewed understanding, belongs a sort of instinctive belief in the absolute existence of nature. In their view man and nature are indissolubly joined. Things are ultimates, and they never look beyond their sphere. The presence of Reason mars this faith. The first effort of thought tends to relax this despotism of the senses which binds us to nature as if we were a part of it, and shows us nature aloof, and, as it were, afloat. Until this higher agency intervened, the animal eye sees, with wonderful accuracy, sharp outlines and colored surfaces. When the eye of Reason opens, to outline and surface are at once added grace and expression. These proceed from imagination and affection, and abate somewhat of the angular distinctness of objects. If the Reason be stimulated to more earnest vision, outlines and surfaces become transparent, and are no longer seen; causes and spirits are seen through them. The best moments of life are these delicious awakenings of the higher powers, and the reverential withdrawing of nature before its God.

Let us proceed to indicate the effects of culture. 1. Our first institution in the Ideal philosophy is a hint from Nature herself.

Nature is made to conspire with spirit to emancipate us. Certain mechanical changes, a small alteration in our local position, apprizes us of a dualism. We are strangely affected by seeing the shore from a moving ship, from a balloon, or through the tints of an unusual sky. The least change in our point of view gives the whole world a pictorial air. A man who seldom rides, needs only to get into a coach and traverse his own town, to turn the street into a puppet-show. The men, the women, — talking, running, bartering, fighting, — the earnest mechanic, the lounger, the beggar, the boys, the dogs, are unrealized at once, or, at least, wholly detached from all relation to the observer, and seen as apparent, not substantial beings. What new thoughts are suggested by seeing a face of country quite familiar, in the rapid movement of the railroad car! Nay, the most wonted objects, (make a very slight change in the point of vision,) please us most. In a camera obscura, the butcher's cart, and the figure

of one of our own family amuse us. So a portrait
of a well-known face gratifies us. Turn the eyes
upside down, by looking at the landscape through
your legs, and how agreeable is the picture, though
you have seen it any time these twenty years !

In these cases, by mechanical means, is suggested
the difference between the observer and the spectacle, — between man and nature. Hence arises a
pleasure mixed with awe; I may say, a low degree
of the sublime is felt, from the fact, probably, that
man is hereby apprized that whilst the world is a
spectacle, something in himself is stable.

2. In a higher manner the poet communicates the
same pleasure. By a few strokes he delineates, as
on air, the sun, the mountain, the camp, the city,
the hero, the maiden, not different from what we
know them, but only lifted from the ground and
afloat before the eye. He unfixes the land and the
sea, makes them revolve around the axis of his primary thought, and disposes them anew. Possessed
himself by a heroic passion, he uses matter as symbols of it. The sensual man conforms thoughts to
things; the poet conforms things to his thoughts.
The one esteems nature as rooted and fast; the
other, as fluid, and impresses his being thereon.
To him, the refractory world is ductile and flexible; he invests dust and stones with humanity, and
makes them the words of the Reason. The Imagi-

nation may be defined to be the use which the Reason makes of the material world. Shakspeare possesses the power of subordinating nature for the purposes of expression, beyond all poets. His imperial muse tosses the creation like a bauble from hand to hand, and uses it to embody any caprice of thought that is uppermost in his mind. The remotest spaces of nature are visited, and the farthest sundered things are brought together, by a subtile spiritual connection. We are made aware that magnitude of material things is relative, and all objects shrink and expand to serve the passion of the poet. Thus in his sonnets, the lays of birds, the scents and dyes of flowers he finds to be the *shadow* of his beloved; time, which keeps her from him, is his *chest ;* the suspicion she has awakened, is her *ornament ;*

> The ornament of beauty is Suspect,
> A crow which flies in heaven's sweetest air.

His passion is not the fruit of chance; it swells, as he speaks, to a city, or a state.

> No, it was builded far from accident;
> It suffers not in smiling pomp, nor falls
> Under the brow of thralling discontent;
> It fears not policy, that heretic,
> That works on leases of short numbered hours,
> But all alone stands hugely politic.

In the strength of his constancy, the Pyramids

seem to him recent and transitory. The freshness
of youth and love dazzles him with its resemblance
to morning;

> Take those lips away
> Which so sweetly were forsworn;
> And those eyes, — the break of day,
> Lights that do mislead the morn.

The wild beauty of this hyperbole, I may say in
passing, it would not be easy to match in literature.

This transfiguration which all material objects
undergo through the passion of the poet, — this
power which he exerts to dwarf the great, to mag-
nify the small, — might be illustrated by a thousand
examples from his Plays. I have before me the
Tempest, and will cite only these few lines.

> ARIEL.   The strong based promontory
> Have I made shake, and by the spurs plucked up
> The pine and cedar.

Prospero calls for music to soothe the frantic
Alonzo, and his companions;

> A solemn air, and the best comforter
> To an unsettled fancy, cure thy brains
> Now useless, boiled within thy skull.

Again;

> The charm dissolves apace,
> And, as the morning steals upon the night,
> Melting the darkness, so their rising senses

> Begin to chase the ignorant fumes that mantle
> Their clearer reason.
>> Their understanding
> Begins to swell: and the approaching tide
> Will shortly fill the reasonable shores
> That now lie foul and muddy.

The perception of real affinities between events (that is to say, of *ideal* affinities, for those only are real), enables the poet thus to make free with the most imposing forms and phenomena of the world, and to assert the predominance of the soul.

3. Whilst thus the poet animates nature with his own thoughts, he differs from the philosopher only herein, that the one proposes Beauty as his main end ; the other Truth. But the philosopher, not less than the poet, postpones the apparent order and relations of things to the empire of thought. " The problem of philosophy," according to Plato, " is, for all that exists conditionally, to find a ground unconditioned and absolute." It proceeds on the faith that a law determines all phenomena, which being known, the phenomena can be predicted. That law, when in the mind, is an idea. Its beauty is infinite. The true philosopher and the true poet are one, and a beauty, which is truth, and a truth, which is beauty, is the aim of both. Is not the charm of one of Plato's or Aristotle's definitions strictly like that of the Antigone of Sophocles ? It

is, in both cases, that a spiritual life has been imparted to nature; that the solid seeming block of matter has been pervaded and dissolved by a thought; that this feeble human being has penetrated the vast masses of nature with an informing soul, and recognized itself in their harmony, that is, seized their law. In physics, when this is attained, the memory disburthens itself of its cumbrous catalogues of particulars, and carries centuries of observation in a single formula.

Thus even in physics, the material is degraded before the spiritual. The astronomer, the geometer, rely on their irrefragable analysis, and disdain the results of observation. The sublime remark of Euler on his law of arches, "This will be found contrary to all experience, yet is true;" had already transferred nature into the mind, and left matter like an outcast corpse.

4. Intellectual science has been observed to beget invariably a doubt of the existence of matter. Turgot said, "He that has never doubted the existence of matter, may be assured he has no aptitude for metaphysical inquiries." It fastens the attention upon immortal necessary uncreated natures, that is, upon Ideas; and in their presence we feel that the outward circumstance is a dream and a shade. Whilst we wait in this Olympus of gods, we think of nature as an appendix to the soul. We ascend

into their region, and know that these are the
thoughts of the Supreme Being. " These are
they who were set up from everlasting, from the
beginning, or ever the earth was. When he prepared the heavens, they were there ; when he established the clouds above, when he strengthened the
fountains of the deep. Then they were by him, as
one brought up with him. Of them took he counsel."

Their influence is proportionate. As objects of
science they are accessible to few men. Yet all
men are capable of being raised by piety or by passion, into their region. And no man touches these
divine natures, without becoming, in some degree,
himself divine. Like a new soul, they renew the
body. We become physically nimble and light-
some ; we tread on air ; life is no longer irksome,
and we think it will never be so. No man fears
age or misfortune or death in their serene company,
for he is transported out of the district of change.
Whilst we behold unveiled the nature of Justice
and Truth, we learn the difference between the absolute and the conditional or relative. We apprehend the absolute. As it were, for the first time, *we
exist*. We become immortal, for we learn that time
and space are relations of matter ; that with a perception of truth or a virtuous will they have no affinity.

5. Finally, religion and ethics, which may be

fitly called the practice of ideas, or the introduc-
tion of ideas into life, have an analogous effect
with all lower culture, in degrading nature and
suggesting its dependence on spirit. Ethics and
religion differ herein ; that the one is the system
of human duties commencing from man ; the other,
from God. Religion includes the personality of
God ; Ethics does not. They are one to our present design. They both put nature under foot. The
first and last lesson of religion is, " The things
that are seen, are temporal ; the things that are unseen, are eternal." It puts an affront upon nature.
It does that for the unschooled, which philosophy
does for Berkeley and Viasa. The uniform language that may be heard in the churches of the
most ignorant sects is, — " Contemn the unsub-
stantial shows of the world ; they are vanities,
dreams, shadows, unrealities ; seek the realities of
religion." The devotee flouts nature. Some theo-
sophists have arrived at a certain hostility and indignation towards matter, as the Manichean and
Plotinus. They distrusted in themselves any looking back to these flesh-pots of Egypt. Plotinus
was ashamed of his body. In short, they might
all say of matter, what Michael Angelo said of external beauty, " It is the frail and weary weed, in
which God dresses the soul which he has called
into time."

It appears that motion, poetry, physical and intellectual science, and religion, all tend to affect our convictions of the reality of the external world. But I own there is something ungrateful in expanding too curiously the particulars of the general proposition, that all culture tends to imbue us with idealism. I have no hostility to nature, but a child's love to it. I expand and live in the warm day like corn and melons. Let us speak her fair. I do not wish to fling stones at my beautiful mother, nor soil my gentle nest. I only wish to indicate the true position of nature in regard to man, wherein to establish man all right education tends; as the ground which to attain is the object of human life, that is, of man's connection with nature. Culture inverts the vulgar views of nature, and brings the mind to call that apparent which it uses to call real, and that real which it uses to call visionary. Children, it is true, believe in the external world. The belief that it appears only, is an afterthought, but with culture this faith will as surely arise on the mind as did the first.

The advantage of the ideal theory over the popular faith is this, that it presents the world in precisely that view which is most desirable to the mind. It is, in fact, the view which Reason, both speculative and practical, that is, philosophy and virtue, take. For seen in the light of thought, the

world always is phenomenal; and virtue subordi-
nates it to the mind. ⸢Idealism sees the world in
God.⸥ It beholds the whole circle of persons and
things, of actions and events, of country and religion, not as painfully accumulated, atom after
atom, act after act, in an aged creeping Past, but
as one vast picture which God paints on the instant eternity for the contemplation of the soul.
Therefore the soul holds itself off from a too trivial
and microscopic study of the universal tablet. It
respects the end too much to immerse itself in the
means. It sees something more important in Christianity than the scandals of ecclesiastical history
or the niceties of criticism; and, very incurious
concerning persons or miracles, and not at all dis-
turbed by chasms of historical evidence, it accepts
from God the phenomenon, as it finds it, as the
pure and awful form of religion in the world. It
is not hot and passionate at the appearance of what
it calls its own good or bad fortune, at the union
or opposition of other persons. No man is its enemy. It accepts whatsoever befalls, as part of its
lesson. It is a watcher more than a doer, and it is
a doer, only that it may the better watch.

CHAPTER VII.

SPIRIT.

It is essential to a true theory of nature and of man, that it should contain somewhat progressive. Uses that are exhausted or that may be, and facts that end in the statement, cannot be all that is true of this brave lodging wherein man is harbored, and wherein all his faculties find appropriate and endless exercise. And all the uses of nature admit of being summed in one, which yields the activity of man an infinite scope. Through all its kingdoms, to the suburbs and outskirts of things, it is faithful to the cause whence it had its origin. It always speaks of Spirit. It suggests the absolute. It is a perpetual effect. It is a great shadow pointing always to the sun behind us.

The aspect of Nature is devout. Like the figure of Jesus, she stands with bended head, and hands folded upon the breast. The happiest man is he who learns from nature the lesson of worship.

Of that ineffable essence which we call Spirit, he that thinks most, will say least. We can foresee God in the coarse, and, as it were, distant phenomena of matter; but when we try to define and describe himself, both language and thought desert us, and we are as helpless as fools and savages. That essence refuses to be recorded in propositions, but when man has worshipped him intellectually, the noblest ministry of nature is to stand as the apparition of God. It is the organ through which the universal spirit speaks to the individual, and strives to lead back the individual to it.

When we consider Spirit, we see that the views already presented do not include the whole circumference of man. We must add some related thoughts.

Three problems are put by nature to the mind; What is matter? Whence is it? and Whereto? The first of these questions only, the ideal theory answers. Idealism saith: matter is a phenomenon, not a substance. Idealism acquaints us with the total disparity between the evidence of our own being and the evidence of the world's being. The one is perfect; the other, incapable of any assurance; the mind is a part of the nature of things; the world is a divine dream, from which we may presently awake to the glories and certainties of day. Idealism is a hypothesis to account for nature by other principles than those of carpentry and chemistry. Yet, if it only deny the existence of matter, it does not satisfy the demands of the spirit. It leaves God out of me. It leaves me in the splendid labyrinth of my perceptions, to wander without end. Then the heart resists it, because it balks the affections in denying substantive being to men and women. Nature is so pervaded with human life that there is something of humanity in all and in every particular. But this theory makes nature foreign to me, and does not account for that consanguinity which we acknowledge to it.

Let it stand then, in the present state of our knowledge, merely as a useful introductory hypothesis, serving to apprise us of the eternal distinction between the soul and the world.

But when, following the invisible steps of thought, we come to inquire, Whence is matter? and Whereto? many truths arise to us out of the recesses of consciousness. We learn that the highest is present to the soul of man; that the dread universal essence, which is not wisdom, or love, or beauty, or power, but all in one, and each entirely, is that for which all things exist, and that by which they are; that spirit creates; that behind nature, throughout nature, spirit is present; one and not compound it does not act upon us from without, that is, in space and time, but spiritually, or through ourselves: therefore, that spirit, that is, the Supreme Being, does not build up nature around us but puts it forth through us, as the life of the tree puts forth new branches and leaves through the pores of the old.   As a plant upon the earth, so a man rests upon the bosom of God; he is nourished by unfailing fountains, and draws at his need inexhaustible power.   Who can set bounds to the possibilities of man?   Once inhale the upper air, being admitted to behold the absolute natures of justice and truth, and we learn that man has access to the entire mind of the Creator, is himself the creator in the finite.   This view, which admonishes me where the sources of wisdom and power lie, and points to virtue as to

> " The golden key
> Which opes the palace of eternity,"

carries upon its face the highest certificate of truth, because it animates me to create my own world through the purification of my soul.

The world proceeds from the same spirit as the body of man.   It is a remoter and inferior incarnation of God, a projection of God in the unconscious.   But it differs from the body in one important respect.   It is not, like that, now subjected to the human will.   Its serene order is inviolable by us.   It is, therefore, to us, the present expositor of the divine mind.   It is a fixed point whereby we may measure our departure.   As we degenerate, the contrast between us and our house is more evident. We are as much strangers in nature as we are aliens from God. We do not understand the notes of birds. The fox and the deer run away from us; the bear and tiger rend us. We do not know the uses of more than a few plants, as corn and the apple, the potato and the vine. Is not the landscape, every glimpse of which hath a grandeur, a face of him? Yet this may show us what discord is between man and nature, for you cannot freely admire a noble landscape if laborers are digging in the field hard by. The poet finds something ridiculous in his delight until he is out of the sight of men.

CHAPTER VIII.

PROSPECTS.

In inquiries respecting the laws of the world and the frame of things, the highest reason is always the truest. That which seems faintly possible, it is so refined, is often faint and dim because it is deepest seated in the mind among the eternal verities. Empirical science is apt to cloud the sight, and by the very knowledge of functions and processes to bereave the student of the manly contemplation of the whole. The savant becomes unpoetic. But the best read naturalist who lends an entire and devout attention to truth, will see that there remains much to learn of his relation to the world, and that it is not to be learned by any addition or subtraction or other comparison of known quantities, but is arrived at by untaught sallies of the spirit, by a continual self-recovery, and by entire humility. He will perceive that there are far more excellent qualities in the student than preciseness and infallibility; that a guess is often more fruitful than an indisputable affirmation, and that a dream may let us deeper into the secret of nature than a hundred concerted experiments.

For the problems to be solved are precisely those which the physiologist and the naturalist omit to state. It is not so pertinent to man to know all the individuals of the animal kingdom, as it is to know whence and whereto is this tyrannizing unity in his constitution, which evermore separates and classifies things, endeavoring to reduce the most diverse to one form. When I behold a rich landscape, it is less to my purpose to recite correctly the order and superposition of the strata, than to know why all thought of multitude is lost in a tranquil sense of unity. I cannot greatly honor minuteness in details, so long as there is no hint to explain the relation between things and thoughts; no ray upon the *metaphysics* of conchology, of botany, of the arts, to show the relation of the forms of flowers, shells, animals, architecture, to the mind, and build science upon ideas. In a cabinet of natural history, we become sensible of a certain occult recognition and sympathy in regard to the most unwieldly and eccentric forms of beast, fish, and insect. The American who has been confined, in his own country, to the sight of buildings designed after foreign models, is surprised on entering York Minster or St. Peter's at Rome, by the feeling that these structures are imitations also, — faint copies of an invisible archetype. Nor has science sufficient humanity, so long as the naturalist overlooks that wonderful congruity which subsists between man and the world ; of which he is lord, not because he is the most subtile inhabitant, but because he is its head and heart, and finds something of himself in every great and small thing, in every mountain stratum, in every new law of color, fact of astronomy, or atmospheric influence which observation or analysis lays open. A perception of this mystery inspires the muse of George Herbert, the beautiful psalmist of the seventeenth century. The following lines are part of his little poem on Man.

> " Man is all symmetry,
> Full of proportions, one limb to another,
> And to all the world besides.
> Each part may call the farthest, brother ;
> For head with foot hath private amity,
> And both with moons and tides.

> " Nothing hath got so far
> But man hath caught and kept it as his prey ;
> His eyes dismount the highest star :
> He is in little all the sphere.
> Herbs gladly cure our flesh, because that they
> Find their acquaintance there.

> " For us, the winds do blow,
> The earth doth rest, heaven move, and fountains flow;
> Nothing we see, but means our good,
> As our delight, or as our treasure;

The whole is either our cupboard of food,
   Or cabinet of pleasure.

   " The stars have us to bed:
Night draws the curtain; which the sun withdraws.
   Music and light attend our head.
   All things unto our flesh are kind,
In their descent and being; to our mind,
   In their ascent and cause.

   " More servants wait on man
Than he 'll take notice of.   In every path,
   He treads down that which doth befriend him
   When sickness makes him pale and wan.
Oh mighty love!   Man is one world, and hath
   Another to attend him."

The perception of this class of truths makes the attraction which draws men to science, but the end is lost sight of in attention to the means.   In view of this half-sight of science, we accept the sentence of Plato, that "poetry comes nearer to vital truth than history."   Every surmise and vaticination of the mind is entitled to a certain respect, and we learn to prefer imperfect theories, and sentences which contain glimpses of truth, to digested systems which have no one valuable suggestion.   A wise writer will feel that the ends of study and composition are best answered by announcing undiscovered regions of thought, and so communicating, through hope, new activity to the torpid spirit.

I shall therefore conclude this essay with some
traditions of man and nature, which a certain poet
sang to me ; and which, as they have always been
in the world, and perhaps reappear to every bard,
may be both history and prophecy.

' The foundations of man are not in matter, but
in spirit. But the element of spirit is eternity. To
it, therefore, the longest series of events, the oldest chronologies are young and recent. In the cycle
of the universal man, from whom the known individuals proceed, centuries are points, and all history
is but the epoch of one degradation.

' We distrust and deny inwardly our sympathy
with nature. We own and disown our relation to
it, by turns. We are like Nebuchadnezzar, de-
throned, bereft of reason, and eating grass like an
ox. But who can set limits to the remedial force of
spirit ?

' A man is a god in ruins. When men are innocent, life shall be longer, and shall pass into the immortal as gently as we awake from dreams. Now,
the world would be insane and rabid, if these dis-
organizations should last for hundreds of years. It
is kept in check by death and infancy. Infancy is
the perpetual Messiah, which comes into the arms
of fallen men, and pleads with them to return to
paradise.

' Man is the dwarf of himself. Once he was permeated and dissolved by spirit. He filled nature with his overflowing currents. Out from him sprang the sun and moon; from man the sun, from woman the moon. The laws of his mind, the periods of his actions externized themselves into day and night, into the year and the seasons. But, having made for himself this huge shell, his waters retired; he no longer fills the veins and veinlets; he is shrunk to a drop. He sees that the structure still fits him, but fits him colossally. Say, rather, once it fitted him, now it corresponds to him from far and on high. He adores timidly his own work. Now is man the follower of the sun, and woman the follower of the moon. Yet sometimes he starts in his slumber, and wonders at himself and his house, and muses strangely at the resemblance betwixt him and it. He perceives that if his law is still paramount, if still he have elemental power, if his word is sterling yet in nature, it is not conscious power, it is not inferior but superior to his will. It is instinct.' Thus my Orphic poet sang.

At present, man applies to nature but half his force. He works on the world with his understanding alone. He lives in it and masters it by a penny-wisdom; and he that works most in it is but a half-man, and whilst his arms are strong and his digestion good, his mind is imbruted, and he is a selfish savage. His relation to nature, his power

over it, is through the understanding, as by ma-
nure ; the economic use of fire, wind, water, and
the mariner's needle ; steam, coal, chemical agriculture ; the repairs of the human body by the dentist
and the surgeon.   This is such a resumption of
power as if a banished king should buy his territories inch by inch, instead of vaulting at once into his
throne.   Meantime, in the thick darkness, there are
not wanting gleams of a better light, — occasional
examples of the action of man upon nature with his
entire force, — with reason as well as understanding.   Such examples are, the traditions of miracles
in the earliest antiquity of all nations ; the history
of Jesus Christ ; the achievements of a principle,
as in religious and political revolutions, and in the
abolition of the slave-trade ; the miracles of enthusiasm, as those reported of Swedenborg, Hohenlohe,
and the Shakers ; many obscure and yet contested
facts, now arranged under the name of Animal
Magnetism ; prayer ; eloquence ; self-healing ; and
the wisdom of children.   These are examples of
Reason's momentary grasp of the sceptre ; the ex-
ertions of a power which exists not in time or space,
but an instantaneous in-streaming causing power.
The difference between the actual and the ideal force
of man is happily figured by the schoolmen, in saying, that the knowledge of man is an evening knowledge, *vespertina cognitio*, but that of God is a
morning knowledge, *matutina cognitio.*

The problem of restoring to the world original and eternal beauty is solved by the redemption of the soul. The ruin or the blank that we see when we look at nature, is in our own eye. The axis of vision is not coincident with the axis of things, and so they appear not transparent but opaque. The reason why the world lacks unity, and lies broken and in heaps, is because man is disunited with himself. He cannot be a naturalist until he satisfies all the demands of the spirit. Love is as much its demand as perception. Indeed, neither can be perfect without the other. In the uttermost meaning of the words, thought is devout, and devotion is thought. Deep calls unto deep. But in actual life, the marriage is not celebrated. There are innocent men who worship God after the tradition of their fathers, but their sense of duty has not yet extended to the use of all their faculties. And there are patient naturalists, but they freeze their subject under the wintry light of the understanding. Is not prayer also a study of truth, — a sally of the soul into the unfound infinite? No man ever prayed heartily without learning something. But when a faithful thinker, resolute to detach every object from personal relations and see it in the light of thought, shall, at the same time, kindle science with the fire of the holiest affections, then will God go forth anew into the creation.

It will not need, when the mind is prepared for study, to search for objects. The invariable mark of wisdom is to see the miraculous in the common. What is a day? What is a year? What is summer? What is woman? What is a child? What is sleep? To our blindness, these things seem unaffecting. We make fables to hide the baldness of the fact and conform it, as we say, to the higher law of the mind. But when the fact is seen under the light of an idea, the gaudy fable fades and shrivels. We behold the real higher law. To the wise, therefore, a fact is true poetry, and the most beautiful of fables. These wonders are brought to our own door. You also are a man. Man and woman and their social life, poverty, labor, sleep, fear, fortune, are known to you. Learn that none of these things is superficial, but that each phenomenon has its roots in the faculties and affections of the mind. Whilst the abstract question occupies your intellect, nature brings it in the concrete to be solved by your hands. It were a wise inquiry for the closet, to compare, point by point, especially at remarkable crises in life, our daily history with the rise and progress of ideas in the mind.

So shall we come to look at the world with new eyes. It shall answer the endless inquiry of the intellect, — What is truth? and of the affections, — What is good? by yielding itself passive to the educated Will. Then shall come to pass what my poet said; ' Nature is not fixed but fluid. Spirit alters, moulds, makes it. The immobility or bruteness of nature is the absence of spirit; to pure spirit it is fluid, it is volatile, it is obedient. Every spirit builds itself a house and beyond its house a world and beyond its world a heaven. Know then that the world exists for you. For you is the phenomenon perfect. What we are, that only can we see. All that Adam had, all that Cæsar could, you have and can do. Adam called his house, heaven and earth; Cæsar called his house, Rome; you perhaps call yours, a cobbler's trade; a hundred acres of ploughed land; or a scholar's garret. Yet line for line and point for point your dominion is as great as theirs, though without fine names. Build therefore your own world. As fast as you conform your life to the pure idea in your mind, that will unfold its great proportions. A correspondent revolution in things will attend the influx of the spirit. So fast will disagreeable appearances, swine, spiders, snakes, pests, mad-houses, prisons, enemies, vanish; they are temporary and shall be no more seen. The sordor and filths of nature, the sun shall dry up and the wind exhale. As when the summer comes from the south the snow-banks melt and the face of the earth becomes green before it, so shall the

advancing spirit create its ornaments along its path,
and carry with it the beauty it visits and the song
which enchants it; it shall draw beautiful faces,
warm hearts, wise discourse, and heroic acts, around
its way, until evil is no more seen.   The kingdom
of man over nature, which cometh not with observation, — a dominion such as now is beyond his
dream of God, — he shall enter without more wonder than the blind man feels who is gradually restored to perfect sight.'

THE AMERICAN SCHOLAR.

AN ORATION DELIVERED BEFORE THE PHI BETA KAPPA SOCIETY, AT CAMBRIDGE, AUGUST 31, 1837.

and soldier. In the *divided* or social state these functions are parcelled out to individuals, each of whom aims to do his stint of the joint work, whilst each other performs his. The fable implies that the individual, to possess himself, must sometimes return from his own labor to embrace all the other laborers. But, unfortunately, this original unit, this fountain of power, has been so distributed to multitudes, has been so minutely subdivided and peddled out, that it is spilled into drops, and cannot be gathered. The state of society is one in which the members have suffered amputation from the trunk, and strut about so many walking monsters, — a good finger, a neck, a stomach, an elbow, but never a man.

Man is thus metamorphosed into a thing, into many things. The planter, who is Man sent out into the field to gather food, is seldom cheered by any idea of the true dignity of his ministry. He sees his bushel and his cart, and nothing beyond, and sinks into the farmer, instead of Man on the farm. The tradesman scarcely ever gives an ideal worth to his work, but is ridden by the routine of his craft, and the soul is subject to dollars. The priest becomes a form ; the attorney a statute-book ; the mechanic a machine ; the sailor a rope of the ship.

In this distribution of functions the scholar is

the delegated intellect. In the right state he is *Man Thinking*. In the degenerate state, when the victim of society, he tends to become a mere thinker, or still worse, the parrot of other men's thinking.

In this view of him, as Man Thinking, the theory of his office is contained. Him Nature solicits with all her placid, all her monitory pictures; him the past instructs; him the future invites. Is not indeed every man a student, and do not all things exist for the student's behoof? And, finally, is not the true scholar the only true master? But the old oracle said, "All things have two handles: beware of the wrong one." In life, too often, the scholar errs with mankind and forfeits his privilege. Let us see him in his school, and consider him in reference to the main influences he receives.

I. The first in time and the first in importance of the influences upon the mind is that of nature. Every day, the sun; and, after sunset, Night and her stars. Ever the winds blow; ever the grass grows. Every day, men and women, conversing, beholding and beholden. The scholar is he of all men whom this spectacle most engages. He must settle its value in his mind. What is nature to him? There is never a beginning, there is never an end, to the inexplicable continuity of this web of God, but always circular power returning into itself. Therein it resembles his own spirit, whose beginning, whose ending, he never can find, — so entire, so boundless. Far too as her splendors shine, system on system shooting like rays, upward, downward, without centre, without circumference, — in the mass and in the particle, Nature hastens to render account of herself to the mind. Classification begins. To the young mind every thing is individual, stands by itself. By and by, it finds how to join two things and see in them one nature ; then three, then three thousand ; and so, tyrannized over by its own unifying instinct, it goes on tying things together, diminishing anomalies, discovering roots running under ground whereby contrary and remote things cohere and flower out from one stem. It presently learns that since the dawn of history there has been a constant accumulation and classifying of facts. But what is classification but the perceiving that these objects are not chaotic, and are not foreign, but have a law which is also a law of the human mind ? The astronomer discovers that geometry, a pure abstraction of the human mind, is the measure of planetary motion. The chemist finds proportions and intelligible method throughout matter ; and science is nothing but the finding of analogy, identity, in the most remote parts. The ambitious soul sits down before each refractory fact ; one after another reduces all strange constitutions, all new powers, to their class and their law, and goes on forever to animate the last fibre of organization, the outskirts of nature, by insight.

Thus to him, to this school-boy under the bending dome of day, is suggested that he and it proceed from one root ; one is leaf and one is flower ; relation, sympathy, stirring in every vein. And what is that root? Is not that the soul of his soul? A thought too bold ; a dream too wild. Yet when this spiritual light shall have revealed the law of more earthly natures, — when he has learned to worship the soul, and to see that the natural philosophy that now is, is only the first gropings of its gigantic hand, he shall look forward to an ever expanding knowledge as to a becoming creator. He shall see that nature is the opposite of the soul, answering to it part for part. One is seal and one is print. Its beauty is the beauty of his own mind. Its laws are the laws of his own mind. Nature then becomes to him the measure of his attainments. So much of nature as he is ignorant of, so much of his own mind does he not yet possess. And, in fine, the ancient precept, " Know thyself," and the modern precept, " Study nature," become at last one maxim.

II. The next great influence into the spirit of the scholar is the mind of the Past, — in whatever form, whether of literature, of art, of institutions, that mind is inscribed. Books are the best type of the influence of the past, and perhaps we shall get at the truth, — learn the amount of this influence more conveniently, — by considering their value alone.

The theory of books is noble. The scholar of the first age received into him the world around; brooded thereon; gave it the new arrangement of his own mind, and uttered it again. It came into him life; it went out from him truth. It came to him short-lived actions; it went out from him immortal thoughts. It came to him business; it went from him poetry. It was dead fact; now, it is quick thought. It can stand, and it can go. It now endures, it now flies, it now inspires. Precisely in proportion to the depth of mind from which it issued, so high does it soar, so long does it sing.

Or, I might say, it depends on how far the process had gone, of transmuting life into truth. In proportion to the completeness of the distillation, so will the purity and imperishableness of the product be. But none is quite perfect. As no air-pump can by any means make a perfect vacuum, so neither can any artist entirely exclude the conventional, the local, the perishable from his book, or write a book of pure thought, that shall be as efficient, in all respects, to a remote posterity, as to contemporaries, or rather to the second age. Each age, it is found, must write its own books; or rather, each generation for the next succeeding. The books of an older period will not fit this.

Yet hence arises a grave mischief. The sacredness which attaches to the act of creation, the act of thought, is transferred to the record. The poet chanting was felt to be a divine man: henceforth the chant is divine also. The writer was a just and wise spirit: henceforward it is settled the book is perfect; as love of the hero corrupts into worship of his statue. Instantly the book becomes noxious: the guide is a tyrant. The sluggish and perverted mind of the multitude, slow to open to the incursions of Reason, having once so opened, having once received this book, stands upon it, and makes an outcry if it is disparaged. Colleges are built on it. Books are written on it by thinkers, not by Man Thinking; by men of talent, that is, who start wrong, who set out from accepted dogmas, not from their own sight of principles. Meek young men grow up in libraries, believing it their duty to accept the views which Cicero, which Locke, which Bacon, have given; forgetful that Cicero, Locke, and Bacon were only young men in libraries when they wrote these books.

Hence, instead of Man Thinking, we have the bookworm. Hence the book - learned class, who value books, as such ; not as related to nature and the human constitution, but as making a sort of Third Estate with the world and the soul. Hence the restorers of readings, the emendators, the bibliomaniacs of all degrees.

Books are the best of things, well used ; abused, among the worst. What is the right use? What is the one end which all means go to effect ? They are for nothing but to inspire. I had better never see a book than to be warped by its attraction clean out of my own orbit, and made a satellite instead of a system. The one thing in the world, of value, is the active soul. This every man is entitled to ; this every man contains within him, although in almost all men obstructed, and as yet unborn. The soul active sees absolute truth and utters truth, or creates. In this action it is genius ; not the privilege of here and there a favorite, but the sound estate of every man. In its essence it is progressive. The book, the college, the school of art, the institution of any kind, stop with some past utterance of genius. This is good, say they, — let us hold by this. They pin me down. They look backward and not forward. But genius looks forward : the eyes of man are set in his forehead, not in his hindhead : man hopes : genius creates.

Whatever talents may be, if the man create not, the pure efflux of the Deity is not his ; — cinders and smoke there may be, but not yet flame. There are creative manners, there are creative actions, and creative words ; manners, actions, words, that is, indicative of no custom or authority, but springing spontaneous from the mind's own sense of good and fair.

On the other part, instead of being its own seer, let it receive from another mind its truth, though it were in torrents of light, without periods of solitude, inquest, and self-recovery, and a fatal disservice is done. Genius is always sufficiently the enemy of genius by over-influence. The literature of every nation bears me witness. The English dramatic poets have Shakspearized now for two hundred years.

Undoubtedly there is a right way of reading, so it be sternly subordinated. Man Thinking must not be subdued by his instruments. Books are for the scholar's idle times. When he can read God directly, the hour is too precious to be wasted in other men's transcripts of their readings. But when the intervals of darkness come, as come they must, — when the sun is hid and the stars withdraw their shining, — we repair to the lamps which were kindled by their ray, to guide our steps to the East again, where the dawn is. We hear, that we may speak. The Arabian proverb says, "A fig tree, looking on a fig tree, becometh fruitful."

It is remarkable, the character of the pleasure we derive from the best books. They impress us with the conviction that one nature wrote and the same reads. We read the verses of one of the great English poets, of Chaucer, of Marvell, of Dryden, with the most modern joy, — with a pleasure, I mean, which is in great part caused by the abstraction of all *time* from their verses. There is some awe mixed with the joy of our surprise, when this poet, who lived in some past world, two or three hundred years ago, says that which lies close to my own soul, that which I also had well-nigh thought and said. But for the evidence thence afforded to the philosophical doctrine of the identity of all minds, we should suppose some preëstablished harmony, some foresight of souls that were to be, and some preparation of stores for their future wants, like the fact observed in insects, who lay up food before death for the young grub they shall never see.

I would not be hurried by any love of system, by any exaggeration of instincts, to underrate the Book. We all know, that as the human body can be nourished on any food, though it were boiled grass and the broth of shoes, so the human mind can be fed by any knowledge. And great and heroic men have existed who had almost no other information than by the printed page. I only would say that it needs a strong head to bear that diet. One must be an inventor to read well. As the proverb says, " He that would bring home the wealth of the Indies, must carry out the wealth of the Indies." There is then creative reading as well as creative writing. When the mind is braced by labor and invention, the page of whatever book we read becomes luminous with manifold allusion. Every sentence is doubly significant, and the sense of our author is as broad as the world. We then see, what is always true, that as the seer's hour of vision is short and rare among heavy days and months, so is its record, perchance, the least part of his volume. The discerning will read, in his Plato or Shakspeare, only that least part, — only the authentic utterances of the oracle ; — all the rest he rejects, were it never so many times Plato's and Shakspeare's.

Of course there is a portion of reading quite indispensable to a wise man. History and exact science he must learn by laborious reading. Colleges, in like manner, have their indispensable office, — to teach elements. But they can only highly serve us when they aim not to drill, but to create ; when they gather from far every ray of various genius to their hospitable halls, and by the concentrated fires, set

the hearts of their youth on flame.) Thought and
knowledge are natures in which apparatus and pretension avail nothing. Gowns and pecuniary foundations, though of towns of gold, can never counter-
vail the least sentence or syllable of wit. Forget this,
and our American colleges will recede in their public importance, whilst they grow richer every year.

III. There goes in the world a notion that the
scholar should be a recluse, a valetudinarian, — as
unfit for any handiwork or public labor as a pen-
knife for an axe. The so-called " practical men "
sneer at speculative men, as if, because they speculate or *see*, they could do nothing. I have heard it
said that the clergy, — who are always, more universally than any other class, the scholars of their
day, — are addressed as women ; that the rough,
spontaneous conversation of men they do not hear,
but only a mincing and diluted speech. They are
often virtually disfranchised ; and indeed there are
advocates for their celibacy. As far as this is true
of the studious classes, it is not just and wise. Action is with the scholar subordinate, but it is essential. Without it he is not yet man. Without it
thought can never ripen into truth. Whilst the
world hangs before the eye as a cloud of beauty, we
cannot even see its beauty. Inaction is cowardice,
but there can be no scholar without the heroic

mind.   The preamble of thought, the transition through which it passes from the unconscious to the conscious, is action.   Only so much do I know, as I have lived.   Instantly we know whose words are loaded with life, and whose not.

The world, — this shadow of the soul, or *other me,* lies wide around.   Its attractions are the keys which unlock my thoughts and make me acquainted with myself.   I run eagerly into this resounding tumult.   I grasp the hands of those next me, and take my place in the ring to suffer and to work, taught by an instinct that so shall the dumb abyss be vocal with speech.   I pierce its order; I dissipate its fear; I dispose of it within the circuit of my expanding life.   So much only of life as I know by experience, so much of the wilderness have I vanquished and planted, or so far have I extended my being, my dominion.   I do not see how any man can afford, for the sake of his nerves and his nap, to spare any action in which he can partake.   It is pearls and rubies to his discourse.   Drudgery, calamity, exasperation, want, are instructors in eloquence and wisdom.   The true scholar grudges every opportunity of action past by, as a loss of power.

It is the raw material out of which the intellect moulds her splendid products.   A strange process too, this by which experience is converted into thought, as a mulberry leaf is converted into satin. The manufacture goes forward at all hours.

The actions and events of our childhood and youth are now matters of calmest observation. They lie like fair pictures in the air. Not so with our recent actions,— with the business which we now have in hand. On this we are quite unable to speculate. Our affections as yet circulate through it. We no more feel or know it than we feel the feet, or the hand, or the brain of our body. The new deed is yet a part of life, — remains for a time immersed in our unconscious life. In some contemplative hour it detaches itself from the life like a ripe fruit, to become a thought of the mind. Instantly it is raised, transfigured; the corruptible has put on incorruption. Henceforth it is an object of beauty, however base its origin and neighborhood. Observe too the impossibility of antedating this act. In its grub state, it cannot fly, it cannot shine, it is a dull grub. But suddenly, without observation, the selfsame thing unfurls beautiful wings, and is an angel of wisdom. So is there no fact, no event, in our private history, which shall not, sooner or later, lose its adhesive, inert form, and astonish us by soaring from our body into the empyrean. Cradle and infancy, school and playground, the fear of boys, and dogs, and ferules, the love of little maids and berries, and many another fact that once filled the whole sky, are gone already; friend and relative, profession and party, town and country, nation and world, must also soar and sing.

Of course, he who has put forth his total strength in fit actions has the richest return of wisdom. I will not shut myself out of this globe of action, and transplant an oak into a flower-pot, there to hunger and pine; nor trust the revenue of some single faculty, and exhaust one vein of thought, much like those Savoyards, who, getting their livelihood by carving shepherds, shepherdesses, and smoking Dutchmen, for all Europe, went out one day to the mountain to find stock, and discovered that they had whittled up the last of their pine-trees. Authors we have, in numbers, who have written out their vein, and who, moved by a commendable prudence, sail for Greece or Palestine, follow the trapper into the prairie, or ramble round Algiers, to replenish their merchantable stock.

If it were only for a vocabulary, the scholar would be covetous of action. Life is our dictionary. Years are well spent in country labors; in town; in the insight into trades and manufactures; in frank intercourse with many men and women; in science; in art; to the one end of mastering in all their facts a language by which to illustrate and embody our perceptions. I learn immediately from any speaker how much he has already lived, through the poverty or the splendor of his speech. Life lies behind us as the quarry from whence we get tiles and copestones for the masonry of to-day. This is the way to learn grammar. Colleges and books only copy the language which the field and the work-yard made.

But the final value of action, like that of books, and better than books, is that it is a resource. That great principle of Undulation in nature, that shows itself in the inspiring and expiring of the breath; in desire and satiety; in the ebb and flow of the sea; in day and night; in heat and cold; and, as yet more deeply ingrained in every atom and every fluid, is known to us under the name of Polarity, — these "fits of easy transmission and reflection," as Newton called them, — are the law of nature because they are the law of spirit.

The mind now thinks, now acts, and each fit reproduces the other. When the artist has exhausted his materials, when the fancy no longer paints, when thoughts are no longer apprehended and books are a weariness, — he has always the resource *to live.* Character is higher than intellect. Thinking is the function. Living is the functionary. The stream retreats to its source. A great soul will be strong to live, as well as strong to think. Does he lack organ or medium to impart his truth? He can still fall back on this elemen-

tal force of living them. This is a total act.
Thinking is a partial act. Let the grandeur of
justice shine in his affairs. Let the beauty of affection cheer his lowly roof. Those " far from
fame," who dwell and act with him, will feel the
force of his constitution in the doings and passages
of the day better than it can be measured by any
public and designed display. Time shall teach him
that the scholar loses no hour which the man lives.
Herein he unfolds the sacred germ of his instinct,
screened from influence. What is lost in seemli-
ness is gained in strength. Not out of those on
whom systems of education have exhausted their
culture, comes the helpful giant to destroy the old
or to build the new, but out of unhandselled savage nature ; out of terrible Druids and Berserkers
come at last Alfred and Shakspeare.

I hear therefore with joy whatever is beginning
to be said of the dignity and necessity of labor to
every citizen. There is virtue yet in the hoe and the
spade, for learned as well as for unlearned hands.
And labor is everywhere welcome; always we are
invited to work ; only be this limitation observed,
that a man shall not for the sake of wider activity sacrifice any opinion to the popular judgments
and modes of action.

I have now spoken of the education of the

scholar by nature, by books, and by action. It remains to say somewhat of his duties.

They are such as become Man Thinking. They may all be comprised in self-trust. The office of the scholar is to cheer, to raise, and to guide men by showing them facts amidst appearances. He plies the slow, unhonored, and unpaid task of observation. Flamsteed and Herschel, in their glazed observatories, may catalogue the stars with the praise of all men, and the results being splendid and useful, honor is sure. But he, in his private observatory, cataloguing obscure and nebulous stars of the human mind, which as yet no man has thought of as such, — watching days and months sometimes for a few facts ; correcting still his old records ; — must relinquish display and immediate fame. In the long period of his preparation he must betray often an ignorance and shiftlessness in popular arts, incurring the disdain of the able who shoulder him aside. Long he must stammer in his speech ; often forego the living for the dead. Worse yet, he must accept, — how often ! poverty and solitude. For the ease and pleasure of treading the old road, accepting the fashions, the education, the religion of society, he takes the cross of making his own, and, of course, the self-accusation, the faint heart, the frequent uncertainty and loss of time, which are the nettles and tangling vines in the way of the self-relying and self-directed; and the state of virtual hostility in which he seems to stand to society, and especially to educated society. For all this loss and scorn, what offset? He is to find consolation in exercising the highest functions of human nature. He is one who raises himself from private considerations and breathes and lives on public and illustrious thoughts. He is the world's eye. He is the world's heart. He is to resist the vulgar prosperity that retrogrades ever to barbarism, by preserving and communicating heroic sentiments, noble biographies, melodious verse, and the conclusions of history. Whatsoever oracles the human heart, in all emergencies, in all solemn hours, has uttered as its commentary on the world of actions, — these he shall receive and impart. And whatsoever new verdict Reason from her inviolable seat pronounces on the passing men and events of to-day, — this he shall hear and promulgate.

These being his functions, it becomes him to feel all confidence in himself, and to defer never to the popular cry. He and he only knows the world. The world of any moment is the merest appearance. Some great decorum, some fetish of a government, some ephemeral trade, or war, or man, is cried up by half mankind and cried down by the other half, as if all depended on this particular up or down.

The odds are that the whole question is not worth the poorest thought which the scholar has lost in listening to the controversy. Let him not quit his belief that a popgun is a popgun, though the ancient and honorable of the earth affirm it to be the crack of doom. In silence, in steadiness, in severe abstraction, let him hold by himself; add observation to observation, patient of neglect, patient of reproach, and bide his own time, — happy enough if he can satisfy himself alone that this day he has seen something truly. Success treads on every right step. For the instinct is sure, that prompts him to tell his brother what he thinks. He then learns that in going down into the secrets of his own mind he has descended into the secrets of all minds. He learns that he who has mastered any law in his private thoughts, is master to that extent of all men whose language he speaks, and of all into whose language his own can be translated. The poet, in utter solitude remembering his spontaneous thoughts and recording them, is found to have recorded that which men in crowded cities find true for them also. The orator distrusts at first the fitness of his frank confessions, his want of knowledge of the persons he addresses, until he finds that he is the complement of his hearers; — that they drink his words because he fulfils for them their own nature; the deeper he dives into his privatest, secretest presentiment, to his wonder he finds this is the most acceptable, most public, and universally true. The people delight in it; the better part of every man feels, This is my music; this is myself.

In self-trust all the virtues are comprehended. Free should the scholar be, — free and brave. Free even to the definition of freedom, " without any hindrance that does not arise out of his own constitution." Brave; for fear is a thing which a scholar by his very function puts behind him. Fear always springs from ignorance. It is a shame to him if his tranquillity, amid dangerous times, arise from the presumption that like children and women his is a protected class; or if he seek a temporary peace by the diversion of his thoughts from politics or vexed questions, hiding his head like an ostrich in the flowering bushes, peeping into microscopes, and turning rhymes, as a boy whistles to keep his courage up. So is the danger a danger still; so is the fear worse. Manlike let him turn and face it. Let him look into its eye and search its nature, inspect its origin, — see the whelping of this lion, — which lies no great way back; he will then find in himself a perfect comprehension of its nature and extent; he will have made his hands meet on the other side, and can henceforth defy it and pass on superior. The world is his who can see through its pretension. What deafness, what stone-blind custom, what overgrown error you behold is there only by sufferance, — by your sufferance. See it to be a lie, and you have already dealt it its mortal blow.

Yes, we are the cowed, — we the trustless. It is a mischievous notion that we are come late into nature ; that the world was finished a long time ago. As the world was plastic and fluid in the hands of God, so it is ever to so much of his attributes as we bring to it. To ignorance and sin, it is flint. They adapt themselves to it as they may ; but in proportion as a man has any thing in him divine, the firmament flows before him and takes his signet and form. Not he is great who can alter matter, but he who can alter my state of mind. They are the kings of the world who give the color of their present thought to all nature and all art, and persuade men by the cheerful serenity of their carrying the matter, that this thing which they do is the apple which the ages have desired to pluck, now at last ripe, and inviting nations to the harvest. The great man makes the great thing. Wherever Macdonald sits, there is the head of the table. Linnæus makes botany the most alluring of studies, and wins it from the farmer and the herb-woman ; Davy, chemistry ; and Cuvier, fossils. The day is always his who works in it with serenity and great aims. The unstable estimates of men crowd to him whose mind is filled with a truth, as the heaped waves of the Atlantic follow the moon.

For this self-trust, the reason is deeper than can
be fathomed, — darker than can be enlightened.
I might not carry with me the feeling of my audience in stating my own belief. But I have already shown the ground of my hope, in adverting
to the doctrine that man is one. I believe man has
been wronged; he has wronged himself. He has
almost lost the light that can lead him back to his
prerogatives. Men are become of no account. Men
in history, men in the world of to-day, are bugs, are
spawn, and are called " the mass" and " the herd."
In a century, in a millennium, one or two men;
that is to say, one or two approximations to the
right state of every man. All the rest behold in
the hero or the poet their own green and crude
being, — ripened; yes, and are content to be less,
so *that* may attain to its full stature. What a testimony, full of grandeur, full of pity, is borne to the
demands of his own nature, by the poor clansman,
the poor partisan, who rejoices in the glory of his
chief. The poor and the low find some amends to
their immense moral capacity, for their acquies-
cence in a political and social inferiority. They
are content to be brushed like flies from the path
of a great person, so that justice shall be done by
him to that common nature which it is the dearest
desire of all to see enlarged and glorified. They
sun themselves in the great man's light, and feel it

to be their own element. They cast the dignity of man from their downtrod selves upon the shoulders of a hero, and will perish to add one drop of blood to make that great heart beat, those giant sinews combat and conquer. He lives for us, and we live in him.

Men such as they are, very naturally seek money or power; and power because it is as good as money, — the "spoils," so called, "of office." And why not? for they aspire to the highest, and this, in their sleep-walking, they dream is highest. Wake them and they shall quit the false good and leap to the true, and leave governments to clerks and desks. This revolution is to be wrought by the gradual domestication of the idea of Culture. The main enterprise of the world for splendor, for extent, is the upbuilding of a man. Here are the materials strewn along the ground. The private life of one man shall be a more illustrious monarchy, more formidable to its enemy, more sweet and serene in its influence to its friend, than any kingdom in history. For a man, rightly viewed, comprehendeth the particular natures of all men. Each philosopher, each bard, each actor has only done for me, as by a delegate, what one day I can do for myself. The books which once we valued more than the apple of the eye, we have quite exhausted. What is that but saying that we have come up with the point of view which the universal mind took through the eyes of one scribe; we have been that man, and have passed on. First, one, then another, we drain all cisterns, and waxing greater by all these supplies, we crave a better and more abundant food. The man has never lived that can feed us ever. The human mind cannot be enshrined in a person who shall set a barrier on any one side to this unbounded, unboundable empire. It is one central fire, which, flaming now out of the lips of Etna, lightens the capes of Sicily, and now out of the throat of Vesuvius, illuminates the towers and vineyards of Naples. It is one light which beams out of a thousand stars. It is one soul which animates all men.

But I have dwelt perhaps tediously upon this abstraction of the Scholar. I ought not to delay longer to add what I have to say of nearer reference to the time and to this country.

Historically, there is thought to be a difference in the ideas which predominate over successive epochs, and there are data for marking the genius of the Classic, of the Romantic, and now of the Reflective or Philosophical age. With the views I have intimated of the oneness or the identity of the mind through all individuals, I do not much dwell on these differences. In fact, I believe each indi-

vidual passes through all three. The boy is a Greek;
the youth, romantic; the adult, reflective. I deny
not however that a revolution in the leading idea
may be distinctly enough traced.

Our age is bewailed as the age of Introversion.
Must that needs be evil? We, it seems, are critical; we are embarrassed with second thoughts; we
cannot enjoy any thing for hankering to know
whereof the pleasure consists; we are lined with
eyes; we see with our feet; the time is infected
with Hamlet's unhappiness, —

"Sicklied o'er with the pale cast of thought."

It is so bad then? Sight is the last thing to be
pitied. Would we be blind? Do we fear lest we
should outsee nature and God, and drink truth
dry? I look upon the discontent of the literary
class as a mere announcement of the fact that they
find themselves not in the state of mind of their
fathers, and regret the coming state as untried; as
a boy dreads the water before he has learned that
he can swim. If there is any period one would desire to be born in, is it not the age of Revolution;
when the old and the new stand side by side and
admit of being compared; when the energies of all
men are searched by fear and by hope; when the
historic glories of the old can be compensated by
the rich possibilities of the new era? This time,

like all times, is a very good one, if we but know what to do with it.

I read with some joy of the auspicious signs of the coming days, as they glimmer already through poetry and art, through philosophy and science, through church and state.

One of these signs is the fact that the same movement which effected the elevation of what was called the lowest class in the state, assumed in literature a very marked and as benign an aspect. Instead of the sublime and beautiful, the near, the low, the common, was explored and poetized. That which had been negligently trodden under foot by those who were harnessing and provisioning themselves for long journeys into far countries, is suddenly found to be richer than all foreign parts. The literature of the poor, the feelings of the child, the philosophy of the street, the meaning of household life, are the topics of the time. It is a great stride. It is a sign, — is it not? of new vigor when the extremities are made active, when currents of warm life run into the hands and the feet. I ask not for the great, the remote, the romantic; what is doing in Italy or Arabia; what is Greek art, or Provençal minstrelsy; I embrace the common, I explore and sit at the feet of the familiar, the low. Give me insight into to-day, and you may have the antique and future worlds. What would we really know the meaning of? The meal in the firkin; the milk in the pan; the ballad in the street; the news of the boat; the glance of the eye; the form and the gait of the body; — show me the ultimate reason of these matters; show me the sublime presence **of** the highest spiritual cause lurking, as always it does lurk, in these suburbs and extremities of nature; let me see every trifle bristling with the polarity that ranges it instantly on an eternal law; and the shop, the plough, and the ledger referred to the like cause by which light undulates and poets sing; — and the world lies no longer a dull miscellany and lumber-room, but has form and order; there is no trifle, there is no puzzle, but one design unites and animates the farthest pinnacle and the lowest trench.

This idea has inspired the genius of Goldsmith, Burns, Cowper, and, in a newer time, of Goethe, Wordsworth, and Carlyle. This idea they have differently followed and with various success. In contrast with their writing, the style of Pope, of Johnson, of Gibbon, looks cold and pedantic. This writing is blood-warm. Man is surprised to *5* find that things near are not less beautiful and wondrous than things remote. The near explains the far. The drop is a small ocean. A man is related to all nature. This perception of the worth of the vulgar is fruitful in discoveries. Goethe, **in** this very thing the most modern of the moderns, has shown us, as none ever did, the genius of the ancients.

There is one man of genius who has done much for this philosophy of life, whose literary value has never yet been rightly estimated; — I mean Emanuel Swedenborg. The most imaginative of men, yet writing with the precision of a mathematician, he endeavored to engraft a purely philosophical Ethics on the popular Christianity of his time. Such an attempt of course must have difficulty which no genius could surmount. But he saw and showed the connection between nature and the affections of the soul. He pierced the emblematic or spiritual character of the visible, audible, tangible world. Especially did his shade-loving muse hover over and interpret the lower parts of nature; he showed the mysterious bond that allies moral evil to the foul material forms, and has given in epical parables a theory of insanity, of beasts, of unclean and fearful things.

Another sign of our times, also marked by an analogous political movement, is the new importance given to the single person. Every thing that tends to insulate the individual, — to surround him with barriers of natural respect, so that each man shall feel the world is his, and man shall treat with man as a sovereign state with a sovereign state,

— tends to true union as well as greatness. " I learned," said the melancholy Pestalozzi, "that no man in God's wide earth is either willing or able to help any other man." Help must come from the bosom alone. The scholar is that man who must take up into himself all the ability of the time, all the contributions of the past, all the hopes of the future. He must be an university of knowledges. If there be one lesson more than another which should pierce his ear, it is, The world is nothing, the man is all ; in yourself is the law of all nature, and you know not yet how a globule of sap ascends ; in yourself slumbers the whole of Reason ; it is for you to know all ; it is for you to dare all. Mr. President and Gentlemen, this confidence in the unsearched might of man belongs, by all motives, by all prophecy, by all preparation, to the American Scholar. We have listened too long to the courtly muses of Europe. The spirit of the American freeman is already suspected to be timid, imitative, tame. Public and private avarice make the air we breathe thick and fat. The scholar is decent, indolent, complaisant. See already the tragic consequence. The mind of this country, taught to aim at low objects, eats upon itself. There is no work for any but the decorous and the complaisant. Young men of the fairest promise, who begin life upon our shores, inflated by the mountain winds, shined upon by all the stars of God, find the earth below not in unison with these, but are hindered from action by the disgust which the principles on which business is managed inspire, and turn drudges, or die of disgust, some of them suicides. What is the remedy? They did not yet see, and thousands of young men as hopeful now crowding to the barriers for the career do not yet see, that if the single man plant himself indomitably on his instincts, and there abide, the huge world will come round to him. Patience, — patience; with the shades of all the good and great for company; and for solace the perspective of your own infinite life; and for work the study and the communication of principles, the making those instincts prevalent, the conversion of the world. Is it not the chief disgrace in the world, not to be an unit; — not to be reckoned one character; — not to yield that peculiar fruit which each man was created to bear, but to be reckoned in the gross, in the hundred, or the thousand, of the party, the section, to which we belong; and our opinion predicted geographically, as the north, or the south? Not so, brothers and friends, — please God, ours shall not be so. We will walk on our own feet; we will work with our own hands; we will speak our own minds. The study of letters shall be no longer a name for pity, for doubt, and for sensual indulgence. The dread of man and the love of man shall be a wall of defence and a wreath of joy around all. A nation of men will for the first time exist, because each believes himself inspired by the Divine Soul which also inspires all men.

AN ADDRESS

DELIVERED BEFORE THE SENIOR CLASS IN DIVINITY COLLEGE,
CAMBRIDGE, SUNDAY EVENING, JULY 15, 1838.

ADDRESS.

IN this refulgent summer, it has been a luxury to draw the breath of life. The grass grows, the buds burst, the meadow is spotted with fire and gold in the tint of flowers. The air is full of birds, and sweet with the breath of the pine, the balm-of-Gilead, and the new hay. Night brings no gloom to the heart with its welcome shade. Through the transparent darkness the stars pour their almost spiritual rays. Man under them seems a young child, and his huge globe a toy. The cool night bathes the world as with a river, and prepares his eyes again for the crimson dawn. The mystery of nature was never displayed more happily. The corn and the wine have been freely dealt to all creatures, and the never-broken silence with which the old bounty goes forward has not yielded yet one word of explanation. One is constrained to respect the perfection of this world in which our senses converse. How wide ; how rich ; what invitation from every property it gives to every faculty of man ! In its fruitful soils ; in its navigable sea ;

in its mountains of metal and stone; in its forests of all woods; in its animals; in its chemical ingredients; in the powers and path of light, heat, attraction and life, it is well worth the pith and heart of great men to subdue and enjoy it. The planters, the mechanics, the inventors, the astronomers, the builders of cities, and the captains, history delights to honor.

But when the mind opens and reveals the laws which traverse the universe and make things what they are, then shrinks the great world at once into a mere illustration and fable of this mind. What am I? and What is? asks the human spirit with a curiosity new-kindled, but never to be quenched. Behold these outrunning laws, which our imperfect apprehension can see tend this way and that, but not come full circle. Behold these infinite relations, so like, so unlike; many, yet one. I would study, I would know, I would admire forever. These works of thought have been the entertainments of the human spirit in all ages.

A more secret, sweet, and overpowering beauty appears to man when his heart and mind open to the sentiment of virtue. Then he is instructed in what is above him. He learns that his being is without bound; that to the good, to the perfect, he is born, low as he now lies in evil and weakness. That which he venerates is still his own, though he has not realized it yet. *He ought.* He knows the sense of that grand word, though his analysis fails to render account of it. When in innocency or when by intellectual perception he attains to say, — "I love the Right; Truth is beautiful within and without forevermore. Virtue, I am thine; save me; use me; thee will I serve, day and night, in great, in small, that I may be not virtuous, but virtue;" — then is the end of the creation answered, and God is well pleased.

The sentiment of virtue is a reverence and delight in the presence of certain divine laws. It perceives that this homely game of life we play, covers, under what seem foolish details, principles that astonish. The child amidst his baubles is learning the action of light, motion, gravity, muscular force; and in the game of human life, love, fear, justice, appetite, man, and God, interact. These laws refuse to be adequately stated. They will not be written out on paper, or spoken by the tongue. They elude our persevering thought; yet we read them hourly in each other's faces, in each other's actions, in our own remorse. The moral traits which are all globed into every virtuous act and thought, —in speech we must sever, and describe or suggest by painful enumeration of many particulars. Yet, as this sentiment is the essence of all religion, let me guide your eye to the precise objects of the sen-

timent, by an enumeration of some of those classes
of facts in which this element is conspicuous.

The intuition of the moral sentiment is an insight of the perfection of the laws of the soul.
These laws execute themselves. They are out of
time, out of space, and not subject to circumstance.
Thus in the soul of man there is a justice whose
retributions are instant and entire. He who does
a good deed is instantly ennobled. He who does
a mean deed is by the action itself contracted. He
who puts off impurity, thereby puts on purity. If
a man is at heart just, then in so far is he God;
the safety of God, the immortality of God, the
majesty of God do enter into that man with justice.
If a man dissemble, deceive, he deceives himself,
and goes out of acquaintance with his own being.
A man in the view of absolute goodness, adores,
with total humility. Every step so downward, is a
step upward. The man who renounces himself,
comes to himself.

See how this rapid intrinsic energy worketh
everywhere, righting wrongs, correcting appearances, and bringing up facts to a harmony with
thoughts. Its operation in life, though slow to the
senses, is at last as sure as in the soul. By it a
man is made the Providence to himself, dispensing
good to his goodness, and evil to his sin. Character
is always known. Thefts never enrich; alms never

impoverish ; murder will speak out of stone walls.
The least admixture of a lie,— for example, the
taint of vanity, any attempt to make a good impression, a favorable appearance, — will instantly vi-
tiate the effect. But speak the truth, and all nature and all spirits help you with unexpected
furtherance. Speak the truth, and all things alive
or brute are vouchers, and the very roots of the
grass underground there do seem to stir and move
to bear you witness. See again the perfection of
the Law as it applies itself to the affections, and
becomes the law of society. As we are, so we associate. The good, by affinity, seek the good ; the
vile, by affinity, the vile. Thus of their own voli-
tion, souls proceed into heaven, into hell.

These facts have always suggested to man the
sublime creed that the world is not the product of
manifold power, but of one will, of one mind ; and
that one mind is everywhere active, in each ray of
the star, in each wavelet of the pool ; and whatever opposes that will is everywhere balked and
baffled, because things are made so, and not otherwise. Good is positive. Evil is merely privative,
not absolute : it is like cold, which is the privation
of heat. All evil is so much death or nonentity.
Benevolence is absolute and real. So much benevolence as a man hath, so much life hath he. For
all things proceed out of this same spirit, which is

differently named love, justice, temperance, in its different applications, just as the ocean receives different names on the several shores which it washes. All things proceed out of the same spirit, and all things conspire with it. Whilst a man seeks good ends, he is strong by the whole strength of nature. In so far as he roves from these ends, he bereaves himself of power, or auxiliaries; his being shrinks out of all remote channels, he becomes less and less, a mote, a point, until absolute badness is absolute death.

The perception of this law of laws awakens in the mind a sentiment which we call the religious sentiment, and which makes our highest happiness. Wonderful is its power to charm and to command. It is a mountain air. It is the embalmer of the world. It is myrrh and storax, and chlorine and rosemary. It makes the sky and the hills sublime, and the silent song of the stars is it. By it is the universe made safe and habitable, not by science or power. Thought may work cold and intransitive in things, and find no end or unity; but the dawn of the sentiment of virtue on the heart, gives and is the assurance that Law is sovereign over all natures; and the worlds, time, space, eternity, do seem to break out into joy.

This sentiment is divine and deifying. It is the beatitude of man. It makes him illimitable.

Through it, the soul first knows itself. It corrects the capital mistake of the infant man, who seeks to be great by following the great, and hopes to derive advantages *from another*, — by showing the fountain of all good to be in himself, and that he, equally with every man, is an inlet into the deeps of Reason. When he says, " I ought ; " when love warms him ; when he chooses, warned from on high, the good and great deed; then, deep melodies wander through his soul from Supreme Wisdom. — Then he can worship, and be enlarged by his worship ; for he can never go behind this sentiment. In the sublimest flights of the soul, rectitude is never surmounted, love is never outgrown.

This sentiment lies at the foundation of society, and successively creates all forms of worship. The principle of veneration never dies out. Man fallen into superstition, into sensuality, is never quite without the visions of the moral sentiment. In like manner, all the expressions of this sentiment are sacred and permanent in proportion to their purity. The expressions of this sentiment affect us more than all other compositions. The sentences of the oldest time, which ejaculate this piety, are still fresh and fragrant. This thought dwelled always deepest in the minds of men in the devout and contemplative East; not alone in Palestine, where it reached its purest expression, but in Egypt, in

Persia, in India, in China. Europe has always owed to oriental genius its divine impulses. What these holy bards said, all sane men found agreeable and true. And the unique impression of Jesus upon mankind, whose name is not so much written as ploughed into the history of this world, is proof of the subtle virtue of this infusion.

Meantime, whilst the doors of the temple stand open, night and day, before every man, and the oracles of this truth cease never, it is guarded by one stern condition; this, namely; it is an intuition. It cannot be received at second hand. Truly speaking, it is not instruction, but provocation, that I can receive from another soul. What he announces, I must find true in me, or reject; and on his word, or as his second, be he who he may, I can accept nothing. On the contrary, the absence of this primary faith is the presence of degradation. As is the flood so is the ebb. Let this faith depart, and the very words it spake and the things it made become false and hurtful. Then falls the church, the state, art, letters, life. The doctrine of the divine nature being forgotten, a sickness infects and dwarfs the constitution. Once man was all; now he is an appendage, a nuisance. And because the indwelling Supreme Spirit cannot wholly be got rid of, the doctrine of it suffers this perversion, that the divine nature is attributed to one or two persons, aud denied to all the rest, and denied with fury. The doctrine of inspiration is lost; the base doctrine of the majority of voices usurps the place of the doctrine of the soul. Miracles, prophecy, poetry, the ideal life, the holy life, exist as ancient history merely; they are not in the belief, nor in the aspiration of society; but, when suggested, seem ridiculous. Life is comic or pitiful as soon as the high ends of being fade out of sight, and man becomes near-sighted, and can only attend to what addresses the senses.

These general views, which, whilst they are general, none will contest, find abundant illustration in the history of religion, and especially in the history of the Christian church. In that, all of us have had our birth and nurture. The truth contained in that, you, my young friends, are now setting forth to teach. As the Cultus, or established worship of the civilized world, it has great historical interest for us. Of its blessed words, which have been the consolation of humanity, you need not that I should speak. I shall endeavor to discharge my duty to you on this occasion, by pointing out two errors in its administration, which daily appear more gross from the point of view we have just now taken.

Jesus Christ belonged to the true race of prophets. He saw with open eye the mystery of the soul. Drawn by its severe harmony, ravished with its beauty, he lived in it, and had his being there. Alone in all history he estimated the greatness of man. One man was true to what is in you and me. He saw that God incarnates himself in man, and evermore goes forth anew to take possession of his World. He said, in this jubilee of sublime emotion, ' I am divine. Through me, God acts; through me, speaks. Would you see God, see me; or see thee, when thou also thinkest as I now think.' But what a distortion did his doctrine and memory suffer in the same, in the next, and the following ages! There is no doctrine of the Reason which will bear to be taught by the Understanding. The understanding caught this high chant from the poet's lips, and said, in the next age, ' This was Jehovah come down out of heaven. I will kill you, if you say he was a man.' The idioms of his language and the figures of his rhetoric have usurped the place of his truth; and churches are not built on his principles, but on his tropes. Christianity became a Mythus, as the poetic teaching of Greece and of Egypt, before. He spoke of miracles; for he felt that man's life was a miracle, and all that man doth, and he knew that this daily miracle shines as the character ascends. But the word Miracle, as pronounced by Christian churches, gives a false impression; it is Monster.

It is not one with the blowing clover and the falling rain.

He felt respect for Moses and the prophets, but no unfit tenderness at postponing their initial revelations to the hour and the man that now is; to the eternal revelation in the heart. Thus was he a true man. Having seen that the law in us is commanding, he would not suffer it to be commanded. Boldly, with hand, and heart, and life, he declared it was God. Thus is he, as I think, the only soul in history who has appreciated the worth of man.

1. In this point of view we become sensible of the first defect of historical Christianity. Historical Christianity has fallen into the error that corrupts all attempts to communicate religion. As it appears to us, and as it has appeared for ages, it is not the doctrine of the soul, but an exaggeration of the personal, the positive, the ritual. It has dwelt, it dwells, with noxious exaggeration about the *person* of Jesus. The soul knows no persons. It invites every man to expand to the full circle of the universe, and will have no preferences but those of spontaneous love. But by this eastern monarchy of a Christianity, which indolence and fear have built, the friend of man is made the injurer of man. The manner in which his name is surrounded with expressions which were once sallies of admiration and love, but are

now petrified into official titles, kills all generous sympathy and liking. All who hear me, feel that the language that describes Christ to Europe and America is not the style of friendship and enthusiasm to a good and noble heart, but is appropriated and formal, — paints a demigod, as the Orientals or the Greeks would describe Osiris or Apollo. Accept the injurious impositions of our early catechetical instruction, and even honesty and self-denial were but splendid sins, if they did not wear the Christian name. One would rather be

" A pagan, suckled in a creed outworn,"

than to be defrauded of his manly right in coming into nature and finding not names and places, not land and professions, but even virtue and truth foreclosed and monopolized. You shall not be a man even. You shall not own the world; you shall not dare and live after the infinite Law that is in you, and in company with the infinite Beauty which heaven and earth reflect to you in all lovely forms; but you must subordinate your nature to Christ's nature; you must accept our interpretations, and take his portrait as the vulgar draw it.

That is always best which gives me to myself. The sublime is excited in me by the great stoical doctrine, Obey thyself. That which shows God in me, fortifies me. That which shows God out of me, makes me a wart and a wen. There is no longer a necessary reason for my being. Already the long shadows of untimely oblivion creep over me, and I shall decease forever.

The divine bards are the friends of my virtue, of my intellect, of my strength. They admonish me that the gleams which flash across my mind are not mine, but God's; that they had the like, and were not disobedient to the heavenly vision. So I love them. Noble provocations go out from them, inviting me to resist evil ; to subdue the world ; and to Be. And thus, by his holy thoughts, Jesus serves us, and thus only. To aim to convert a man by miracles, is a profanation of the soul. A true conversion, a true Christ, is now, as always, to be made by the reception of beautiful sentiments. It is true that a great and rich soul, like his, falling among the simple, does so preponderate, that, as his did, it names the world. The world seems to them to exist for him, and they have not yet drunk so deeply of his sense as to see that only by coming again to themselves, or to God in themselves, can they grow forevermore. It is a low benefit to give me something ; it is a high benefit to enable me to do somewhat of myself. The time is coming when all men will see that the gift of God to the soul is not a vaunting, overpowering, excluding sanctity, but a sweet, natural goodness, a goodness like thine and mine, and that so invites thine and mine to be and to grow.

The injustice of the vulgar tone of preaching is not less flagrant to Jesus than to the souls which it profanes. The preachers do not see that they make his gospel not glad, and shear him of the locks of beauty and the attributes of heaven. When I see a majestic Epaminondas, or Washington; when I see among my contemporaries a true orator, an upright judge, a dear friend; when I vibrate to the melody and fancy of a poem; I see beauty that is to be desired. And so lovely, and with yet more entire consent of my human being, sounds in my ear the severe music of the bards that have sung of the true God in all ages. Now do not degrade the life and dialogues of Christ out of the circle of this charm, by insulation and peculiarity. Let them lie as they befel, alive and warm, part of human life and of the landscape and of the cheerful day.

2. The second defect of the traditionary and limited way of using the mind of Christ, is a consequence of the first; this, namely; that the Moral Nature, that Law of laws whose revelations introduce greatness, — yea, God himself, — into the open soul, is not explored as the fountain of the established teaching in society. Men have come to speak of the revelation as somewhat long ago given and done, as if God were dead. The injury to

faith throttles the preacher; and the goodliest of institutions becomes an uncertain and inarticulate voice.

It is very certain that it is the effect of conversation with the beauty of the soul, to beget a desire and need to impart to others the same knowledge and love. If utterance is denied, the thought lies like a burden on the man. Always the seer is a sayer. Somehow his dream is told; somehow he publishes it with solemn joy: sometimes with pencil on canvas, sometimes with chisel on stone, sometimes in towers and aisles of granite, his soul's worship is builded; sometimes in anthems of indefinite music; but clearest and most permanent, in words.

The man enamored of this excellency becomes its priest or poet. The office is coeval with the world. But observe the condition, the spiritual limitation of the office. The spirit only can teach. Not any profane man, not any sensual, not any liar, not any slave can teach, but only he can give, who has; he only can create, who is. The man on whom the soul descends, through whom the soul speaks, alone can teach. Courage, piety, love, wisdom, can teach; and every man can open his door to these angels, and they shall bring him the gift of tongues. But the man who aims to speak as books enable, as synods use, as the fashion guides, and as interest commands, babbles. Let him hush.

To this holy office you propose to devote your-selves. I wish you may feel your call in throbs of desire and hope. The office is the first in the world. It is of that reality that it cannot suffer the deduction of any falsehood. And it is my duty to say to you that the need was never greater of new revelation than now. From the views I have already expressed, you will infer the sad convic-tion, which I share, I believe, with numbers, of the universal decay and now almost death of faith in society. The soul is not preached. The Church seems to totter to its fall, almost all life extinct. On this occasion, any complaisance would be crim-inal which told you, whose hope and commission it is to preach the faith of Christ, that the faith of Christ is preached.

It is time that this ill-suppressed murmur of all thoughtful men against the famine of our churches; — this moaning of the heart because it is bereaved of the consolation, the hope, the grandeur that come alone out of the culture of the moral nature, — should be heard through the sleep of indolence, and over the din of routine. This great and per-petual office of the preacher is not discharged. Preaching is the expression of the moral sentiment in application to the duties of life. In how many churches, by how many prophets, tell me, is man made sensible that he is an infinite Soul; that the

earth and heavens are passing into his mind ; that
he is drinking forever the soul of God ? Where
now sounds the persuasion, that by its very melody
imparadises my heart, and so affirms its own origin
in heaven ? Where shall I hear words such as in
elder ages drew men to leave all and follow, —
father and mother, house and land, wife and child ?
Where shall I hear these august laws of moral being so pronounced as to fill my ear, and I feel ennobled by the offer of my uttermost action and passion ? The test of the true faith, certainly, should
be its power to charm and command the soul, as
the laws of nature control the activity of the hands,
— so commanding that we find pleasure and honor
in obeying. The faith should blend with the light
of rising and of setting suns, with the flying cloud,
the singing bird, and the breath of flowers. But
now the priest's Sabbath has lost the splendor of
nature ; it is unlovely ; we are glad when it is done ;
we can make, we do make, even sitting in our
pews, a far better, holier, sweeter, for ourselves.

Whenever the pulpit is usurped by a formalist,
then is the worshipper defrauded and disconsolate.
We shrink as soon as the prayers begin, which do
not uplift, but smite and offend us. We are fain
to wrap our cloaks about us, and secure, as best we
can, a solitude that hears not. I once heard a
preacher who sorely tempted me to say I would go

to church no more.   Men go, thought I, where
they are wont to go, else had no soul entered the
temple in the afternoon.   A snow-storm was falling around us.   The snow-storm was real, the
preacher merely spectral, and the eye felt the sad
contrast in looking at him, and then out of the
window behind him into the beautiful meteor of
the snow.   He had lived in vain.   He had no one
word intimating that he had laughed or wept,
was married or in love, had been commended, or
cheated, or chagrined.   If he had ever lived and
acted, we were none the wiser for it.   The capital
secret of his profession, namely, to convert life
into truth, he had not learned.   Not one fact in
all his experience had he yet imported into his doctrine.   This man had ploughed and planted and
talked and bought and sold; he had read books;
he had eaten and drunken; his head aches, his
heart throbs; he smiles and suffers; yet was there
not a surmise, a hint, in all the discourse, that he
had ever lived at all.   Not a line did he draw out
of real history.   The true preacher can be known
by this, that he deals out to the people his life, —
life passed through the fire of thought.   But of the
bad preacher, it could not be told from his sermon
what age of the world he fell in; whether he had a
father or a child; whether he was a freeholder or
a pauper; whether he was a citizen or a country-

man; or any other fact of his biography. It seemed strange that the people should come to church. It seemed as if their houses were very unentertaining, that they should prefer this thoughtless clamor. It shows that there is a commanding attraction in the moral sentiment, that can lend a faint tint of light to dulness and ignorance coming in its name and place. The good hearer is sure he has been touched sometimes; is sure there is somewhat to be reached, and some word that can reach it. When he listens to these vain words, he comforts himself by their relation to his remembrance of better hours, and so they clatter and echo unchallenged.

I am not ignorant that when we preach unworthily, it is not always quite in vain. There is a good ear, in some men, that draws supplies to virtue out of very indifferent nutriment. There is poetic truth concealed in all the common-places of prayer and of sermons, and though foolishly spoken, they may be wisely heard; for each is some select expression that broke out in a moment of piety from some stricken or jubilant soul, and its excellency made it remembered. The prayers and even the dogmas of our church are like the zodiac of Denderah and the astronomical monuments of the Hindoos, wholly insulated from anything now extant in the life and business of the people. They mark the

height to which the waters once rose. But this docility is a check upon the mischief from the good
and devout. In a large portion of the community,
the religious service gives rise to quite other thoughts
and emotions. We need not chide the negligent
servant. We are struck with pity, rather, at the
swift retribution of his sloth. Alas for the unhappy man that is called to stand in the pulpit, and
not give bread of life. Everything that befalls, accuses him. Would he ask contributions for the
missions, foreign or domestic? Instantly his face
is suffused with shame, to propose to his parish that
they should send money a hundred or a thousand
miles, to furnish such poor fare as they have at
home and would do well to go the hundred or the
thousand miles to escape. Would he urge people
to a godly way of living; — and can he ask a
fellow-creature to come to Sabbath meetings, when
he and they all know what is the poor uttermost
they can hope for therein? Will he invite them
privately to the Lord's Supper? He dares not. If
no heart warm this rite, the hollow, dry, creaking
formality is too plain than that he can face a man
of wit and energy and put the invitation without
terror. In the street, what has he to say to the
bold village blasphemer? The village blasphemer
sees fear in the face, form, and gait of the minister.

Let me not taint the sincerity of this plea by any oversight of the claims of good men. I know and honor the purity and strict conscience of numbers of the clergy. What life the public worship retains, it owes to the scattered company of pious men, who minister here and there in the churches, and who, sometimes accepting with too great tenderness the tenet of the elders, have not accepted from others, but from their own heart, the genuine impulses of virtue, and so still command our love and awe, to the sanctity of character. Moreover, the exceptions are not so much to be found in a few eminent preachers, as in the better hours, the truer inspirations of all, — nay, in the sincere moments of every man. But, with whatever exception, it is still true that tradition characterizes the preaching of this country; that it comes out of the memory, and not out of the soul; that it aims at what is usual, and not at what is necessary and eternal; that thus historical Christianity destroys the power of preaching, by withdrawing it from the exploration of the moral nature of man; where the sublime is, where are the resources of astonishment and power. What a cruel injustice it is to that Law, the joy of the whole earth, which alone can make thought dear and rich; that Law whose fatal sureness the astronomical orbits poorly emulate; — that it is travestied and depreciated, that it is behooted and behowled, and not a trait, not a word of it articulated. The pulpit in losing sight of this Law, loses its reason, and gropes after it knows not what. And for want of this culture the soul of the community is sick and faithless. It wants nothing so much as a stern, high, stoical, Christian discipline, to make it know itself and the divinity that speaks through it. Now man is ashamed of himself; he skulks and sneaks through the world, to be tolerated, to be pitied, and scarcely in a thousand years does any man dare to be wise and good, and so draw after him the tears and blessings of his kind.

Certainly there have been periods when, from the inactivity of the intellect on certain truths, a greater faith was possible in names and persons. The Puritans in England and America found in the Christ of the Catholic Church and in the dogmas inherited from Rome, scope for their austere piety and their longings for civil freedom. But their creed is passing away, and none arises in its room. I think no man can go with his thoughts about him into one of our churches, without feeling that what hold the public worship had on men is gone, or going. It has lost its grasp on the affection of the good and the fear of the bad. In the country, neighborhoods, half parishes are *signing off*, to use the local term. It is already beginning to indicate character and religion to withdraw from the religious meetings.

I have heard a devout person, who prized the Sabbath, say in bitterness of heart, " On Sundays, it
seems wicked to go to church." And the motive
that holds the best there is now only a hope and
a waiting. What was once a mere circumstance,
that the best and the worst men in the parish, the
poor and the rich, the learned and the ignorant,
young and old, should meet one day as fellows in
one house, in sign of an equal right in the soul, has
come to be a paramount motive for going thither.

My friends, in these two errors, I think, I find the
causes of a decaying church and a wasting unbelief.
And what greater calamity can fall upon a nation
than the loss of worship? Then all things go to decay. Genius leaves the temple to haunt the senate or the market. Literature becomes frivolous.
Science is cold. The eye of youth is not lighted by
the hope of other worlds, and age is without honor.
Society lives to trifles, and when men die we do not
mention them.

And now, my brothers, you will ask, What in
these desponding days can be done by us? The
remedy is already declared in the ground of our
complaint of the Church. We have contrasted the
Church with the Soul. In the soul then let the redemption be sought. Wherever a man comes, there
comes revolution. The old is for slaves. When a
man comes, all books are legible, all things trans-

parent, all religions are forms. He is religious. Man is the wonderworker. He is seen amid miracles. All men bless and curse. He saith yea and nay, only. The stationariness of religion; the assumption that the age of inspiration is past, that the Bible is closed ; the fear of degrading the character of Jesus by representing him as a man ; — indicate with sufficient clearness the falsehood of our theology. It is the office of a true teacher to show us that God is, not was ; that He speaketh, not spake. The true Christianity, — a faith like Christ's in the infinitude of man, — is lost. None believeth in the soul of man, but only in some man or person old and departed. Ah me ! no man goeth alone. All men go in flocks to this saint or that poet, avoiding the God who seeth in secret. They cannot see in secret ; they love to be blind in public. They think society wiser than their soul, and know not that one soul, and their soul, is wiser than the whole world. See how nations and races flit by on the sea of time and leave no ripple to tell where they floated or sunk, and one good soul shall make the name of Moses, or of Zeno, or of Zoroaster, reverend forever. None assayeth the stern ambition to be the Self of the nation and of nature, but each would be an easy secondary to some Christian scheme, or sectarian connection, or some eminent man. Once leave your own knowledge of God, your own sentiment, and take secondary knowledge, as St. Paul's, or George Fox's, or Swedenborg's, and you get wide from God with every year this secondary form lasts, and if, as now, for centuries, — the chasm yawns to that breadth, that men can scarcely be convinced there is in them anything divine.

Let me admonish you, first of all, to go alone ; to refuse the good models, even those which are sacred in the imagination of men, and dare to love God without mediator or veil. Friends enough you shall find who will hold up to your emulation Wesleys and Oberlins, Saints and Prophets. Thank God for these good men, but say, ' I also am a man.' Imitation cannot go above its model. The imitator dooms himself to hopeless mediocrity. The inventor did it because it was natural to him, and so in him it has a charm. In the imitator something else is natural, and he bereaves himself of his own beauty, to come short of another man's.

Yourself a newborn bard of the Holy Ghost, cast behind you all conformity, and acquaint men at first hand with Deity. Look to it first and only, that fashion, custom, authority, pleasure, and money, are nothing to you, — are not bandages over your eyes, that you cannot see, — but live with the privilege of the immeasurable mind. Not too anxious to visit periodically all families and each family in your

parish connection, — when you meet one of these
men or women, be to them a divine man; be to
them thought and virtue; let their timid aspirations
find in you a friend; let their trampled instincts
be genially tempted out in your atmosphere; let
their doubts know that you have doubted, and their
wonder feel that you have wondered. By trusting
your own heart, you shall gain more confidence in
other men. For all our penny-wisdom, for all our
soul-destroying slavery to habit, it is not to be
doubted that all men have sublime thoughts; that
all men value the few real hours of life; they love
to be heard; they love to be caught up into the
vision of principles. We mark with light in the
memory the few interviews we have had, in the
dreary years of routine and of sin, with souls that
made our souls wiser; that spoke what we thought;
that told us what we knew; that gave us leave to
be what we inly were. Discharge to men the
priestly office, and, present or absent, you shall be
followed with their love as by an angel.

And, to this end, let us not aim at common degrees of merit. Can we not leave, to such as love
it, the virtue that glitters for the commendation of
society, and ourselves pierce the deep solitudes of
absolute ability and worth? We easily come up
to the standard of goodness in society. Society's
praise can be cheaply secured, and almost all men

are content with those easy merits ; but the instant effect of conversing with God will be to put them away. There are persons who are not actors, not speakers, but influences ; persons too great for fame, for display ; who disdain eloquence ; to whom all we call art and artist, seems too nearly allied to show and by-ends, to the exaggeration of the finite and selfish, and loss of the universal. The orators, the poets, the commanders encroach on us only as fair women do, by our allowance and homage. Slight them by preoccupation of mind, slight them, as you can well afford to do, by high and universal aims, and they instantly feel that you have right, and that it is in lower places that they must shine. They also feel your right ; for they with you are open to the influx of the all-knowing Spirit, which annihilates before its broad noon the little shades and gradations of intelligence in the compositions we call wiser and wisest.

In such high communion let us study the grand strokes of rectitude : a bold benevolence, an independence of friends, so that not the unjust wishes of those who love us shall impair our freedom, but we shall resist for truth's sake the freest flow of kindness, and appeal to sympathies far in advance ; and, — what is the highest form in which we know this beautiful element, — a certain solidity of merit, that has nothing to do with opinion, and which is so essentially and manifestly virtue, that it is taken for granted that the right, the brave, the generous step will be taken by it, and nobody thinks of commending it. You would compliment a coxcomb doing a good act, but you would not praise an angel. The silence that accepts merit as the most natural thing in the world, is the highest applause. Such souls, when they appear, are the Imperial Guard of Virtue, the perpetual reserve, the dictators of fortune. One needs not praise their courage, — they are the heart and soul of nature. O my friends, there are resources in us on which we have not drawn. There are men who rise refreshed on hearing a threat ; men to whom a crisis which intimidates and paralyzes the majority, — demanding not the faculties of prudence and thrift, but comprehension, immovableness, the readiness of sacrifice, — comes graceful and beloved as a bride. Napoleon said of Massena, that he was not himself until the battle began to go against him ; then, when the dead began to fall in ranks around him, awoke his powers of combination, and he put on terror and victory as a robe. So it is in rugged crises, in unweariable endurance, and in aims which put sympathy out of question, that the angel is shown. But these are heights that we can scarce remember and look up to without contrition and shame. Let us thank God that such things exist.

And now let us do what we can to rekindle the smouldering, nigh quenched fire on the altar. The evils of the church that now is are manifest. The question returns, What shall we do? I confess, all attempts to project and establish a Cultus with new rites and forms, seem to me vain. Faith makes us, and not we it, and faith makes its own forms. All attempts to contrive a system are as cold as the new worship introduced by the French to the goddess of Reason, — to-day, pasteboard and filigree, and ending to-morrow in madness and murder. Rather let the breath of new life be breathed by you through the forms already existing. For if once you are alive, you shall find they shall become plastic and new. The remedy to their deformity is first, soul, and second, soul, and evermore, soul. A whole popedom of forms one pulsation of virtue can uplift and vivify. Two inestimable advantages Christianity has given us; first the Sabbath, the jubilee of the whole world, whose light dawns welcome alike into the closet of the philosopher, into the garret of toil, and into prison-cells, and everywhere suggests, even to the vile, the dignity of spiritual being. Let it stand forevermore, a temple, which new love, new faith, new sight shall restore to more than its first splendor to mankind. And secondly, the institution of preaching, — the speech of man to men, — essentially the most flexible of all organs, of all forms. What hinders that now, everywhere, in pulpits, in lecture-rooms, in houses, in fields, wherever the invitation of men or your own occasions lead you, you speak the very truth, as your life and conscience teach it, and cheer the waiting, fainting hearts of men with new hope and new revelation?

I look for the hour when that supreme Beauty which ravished the souls of those eastern men, and chiefly of those Hebrews, and through their lips spoke oracles to all time, shall speak in the West also. The Hebrew and Greek Scriptures contain immortal sentences, that have been bread of life to millions. But they have no epical integrity; are fragmentary; are not shown in their order to the intellect. I look for the new Teacher that shall follow so far those shining laws that he shall see them come full circle; shall see their rounding complete grace; shall see the world to be the mirror of the soul; shall see the identity of the law of gravitation with purity of heart; and shall show that the Ought, that Duty, is one thing with Science, with Beauty, and with Joy.

LITERARY ETHICS.

AN ORATION DELIVERED BEFORE THE LITERARY SOCIETIES OF
DARTMOUTH COLLEGE, JULY 24, 1838.

ORATION.

Gentlemen,

The invitation to address you this day, with which you have honored me, was a call so welcome that I made haste to obey it. A summons to celebrate with scholars a literary festival, is so alluring to me as to overcome the doubts I might well entertain of my ability to bring you any thought worthy of your attention. I have reached the middle age of man ; yet I believe I am not less glad or sanguine at the meeting of scholars, than when, a boy, I first saw the graduates of my own College assembled at their anniversary. Neither years nor books have yet availed to extirpate a prejudice then rooted in me, that a scholar is the favorite of Heaven and earth, the excellency of his country, the happiest of men. His duties lead him directly into the holy ground where other men's aspirations only point. His successes are occasions of the purest joy to all men. Eyes is he to the blind ; feet is he to the lame. His failures, if he is worthy, are inlets to higher advantages. And because the scholar by every thought he thinks extends his dominion into the general mind of men, he is not one, but many. The few scholars in each country, whose genius I know, seem to me not individuals, but societies; and when events occur of great import, I count over these representatives of opinion, whom they will affect, as if I were counting nations. And even if his results were incommunicable; if they abode in his own spirit; the intellect hath somewhat so sacred in its possessions that the fact of his existence and pursuits would be a happy omen.

Meantime I know that a very different estimate of the scholar's profession prevails in this country, and the importunity, with which society presses its claim upon young men, tends to pervert the views of the youth in respect to the culture of the intellect. Hence the historical failure, on which Europe and America have so freely commented. This country has not fulfilled what seemed the reasonable expectation of mankind. Men looked, when all feudal straps and bandages were snapped asunder, that nature, too long the mother of dwarfs, should reimburse itself by a brood of Titans, who should laugh and leap in the continent, and run up the mountains of the West with the errand of genius and of love. But the mark of American merit in painting, in sculpture, in poetry, in fiction, in eloquence, seems to be a certain grace without grandeur, and itself not new but derivative, a vase of fair outline, but empty, — which whoso sees may fill with what wit and character is in him, but which does not, like the charged cloud, overflow with terrible beauty, and emit lightnings on all beholders.

I will not lose myself in the desultory questions, what are the limitations, and what the causes of the fact. It suffices me to say, in general, that the diffidence of mankind in the soul has crept over the American mind; that men here, as elsewhere, are indisposed to innovation, and prefer any antiquity, any usage, any livery productive of ease or profit, to the unproductive service of thought.

Yet in every sane hour the service of thought appears reasonable, the despotism of the senses insane. The scholar may lose himself in schools, in words, and become a pedant; but when he comprehends his duties he above all men is a realist, and converses with things. For the scholar is the student of the world; and of what worth the world is, and with what emphasis it accosts the soul of man, such is the worth, such the call of the scholar.

The want of the times and the propriety of this anniversary concur to draw attention to the doctrine of Literary Ethics. What I have to say on that doctrine distributes itself under the topics of the resources, the subject, and the discipline of the scholar.

I. The resources of the scholar are proportioned
to his confidence in the attributes of the Intellect.
The resources of the scholar are co-extensive with
nature and truth, yet can never be his unless claimed
by him with an equal greatness of mind. He cannot know them until he has beheld with awe the infinitude and impersonality of the intellectual power.
When he has seen that it is not his, nor any man's,
but that it is the soul which made the world, and
that it is all accessible to him, he will know that he,
as its minister, may rightfully hold all things subordinate and answerable to it. A divine pilgrim
in nature, all things attend his steps. Over him
stream the flying constellations; over him streams
Time, as they, scarcely divided into months and
years. He inhales the year as a vapor: its fragrant
mid-summer breath, its sparkling January heaven.
And so pass into his mind, in bright transfiguration, the grand events of history, to take a new
order and scale from him. He is the world; and
the epochs and heroes of chronology are pictorial
images, in which his thoughts are told. There is
no event but sprung somewhere from the soul of
man; and therefore there is none but the soul of
man can interpret. Every presentiment of the
mind is executed somewhere in a gigantic fact.
What else is Greece, Rome, England, France, St.
Helena? What else are churches, literatures, and

empires? The new man must feel that he is new, and has not come into the world mortgaged to the opinions and usages of Europe, and Asia, and Egypt. The sense of spiritual independence is like the lovely varnish of the dew, whereby the old, hard, peaked earth and its old self-same productions are made new every morning, and shining with the last touch of the artist's hand. A false humility, a complaisance to reigning schools or to the wisdom of antiquity, must not defraud me of supreme possession of this hour. If any person have less love of liberty and less jealousy to guard his integrity, shall he therefore dictate to you and me? Say to such doctors, We are thankful to you, as we are to history, to the pyramids, and the authors; but now our day is come; we have been born out of the eternal silence; and now will we live, — live for ourselves, — and not as the pall-bearers of a funeral, but as the upholders and creators of our age; and neither Greece nor Rome, nor the three Unities of Aristotle, nor the three Kings of Cologne, nor the College of the Sorbonne, nor the Edinburgh Review is to command any longer. Now that we are here we will put our own interpretation on things, and our own things for interpretation. Please himself with complaisance who will, — for me, things must take my scale, not I theirs. I will say with the warlike king, "God gave me this crown, and the whole world shall not take it away."

The whole value of history, of biography, is to increase my self-trust, by demonstrating what man can be and do. This is the moral of the Plutarchs, the Cudworths, the Tennemanns, who give us the story of men or of opinions. Any history of philosophy fortifies my faith, by showing me that what high dogmas I had supposed were the rare and late fruit of a cumulative culture, and only now possible to some recent Kant or Fichte, — were the prompt improvisations of the earliest inquirers; of Parmenides, Heraclitus, and Xenophanes. In view of these students, the soul seems to whisper, 'There is a better way than this indolent learning of another. Leave me alone; do not teach me out of Leibnitz or Schelling, and I shall find it all out myself.'

Still more do we owe to biography the fortification of our hope. If you would know the power of character, see how much you would impoverish the world if you could take clean out of history the lives of Milton, Shakspeare, and Plato, — these three, and cause them not to be. See you not how much less the power of man would be? I console myself in the poverty of my thoughts, in the paucity of great men, in the malignity and dulness of the nations, by falling back on these sublime recollections, and seeing what the prolific soul could beget on actual nature; — seeing that Plato was, and Shakspeare, and Milton, — three irrefragable facts. Then I dare; I also will essay to be. The humblest, the most hopeless, in view of these radiant facts, may now theorize and hope. In spite of all the rueful abortions that squeak and gibber in the street, in spite of slumber and guilt, in spite of the army, the bar-room, and the jail, *have been* these glorious manifestations of the mind; and I will thank my great brothers so truly for the admonition of their being, as to endeavor also to be just and brave, to aspire and to speak. Plotinus too, and Spinoza, and the immortal bards of philosophy, — that which they have written out with patient courage, makes me bold. No more will I dismiss, with haste, the visions which flash and sparkle across my sky; but observe them, approach them, domesticate them, brood on them, and draw out of the past, genuine life for the present hour.

To feel the full value of these lives, as occasions of hope and provocation, you must come to know that each admirable genius is but a successful diver in that sea whose floor of pearls is all your own. The impoverishing philosophy of ages has laid stress on the distinctions of the individual, and not on the universal attributes of man. The youth, intoxicated with his admiration of a hero, fails to see that it is only a projection of his own soul which he admires. In solitude, in a remote vil-

lage, the ardent youth loiters and mourns. With
inflamed eye, in this sleeping wilderness, he has
read the story of the Emperor Charles the Fifth,
until his fancy has brought home to the surrounding woods, the faint roar of cannonades in the
Milanese, and marches in Germany. He is curious concerning that man's day. What filled it?
the crowded orders, the stern decisions, the foreign despatches, the Castilian etiquette? The soul
answers — Behold his day here! In the sighing of
these woods, in the quiet of these gray fields, in
the cool breeze that sings out of these northern
mountains; in the workmen, the boys, the maidens you meet, — in the hopes of the morning, the
ennui of noon, and sauntering of the afternoon; in
the disquieting comparisons; in the regrets at want
of vigor; in the great idea and the puny execu-
tion; — behold Charles the Fifth's day; another,
yet the same; behold Chatham's, Hampden's, Bay-
ard's, Alfred's, Scipio's, Pericles's day, — day of
all that are born of women. The difference of circumstance is merely costume. I am tasting the
self-same life, — its sweetness, its greatness, its
pain, which I so admire in other men. Do not
foolishly ask of the inscrutable, obliterated past,
what it cannot tell, — the details of that nature, of
that day, called Byron, or Burke; — but ask it of
the enveloping Now; the more quaintly you in-

spect its evanescent beauties, its wonderful details, its spiritual causes, its astounding whole, — so much the more you master the biography of this hero, and that, and every hero. Be lord of a day, through wisdom and justice, and you can put up your history books.

An intimation of these broad rights is familiar in the sense of injury which men feel in the assumption of any man to limit their possible progress. We resent all criticism which denies us anything that lies in our line of advance. Say to the man of letters that he cannot paint a Transfiguration, or build a steamboat, or be a grand-marshal, — and he will not seem to himself depreciated. But deny to him any quality of literary or metaphysical power, and he is piqued. Concede to him genius, which is a sort of Stoical *plenum* annulling the comparative, and he is content; but concede him talents never so rare, denying him genius, and he is aggrieved. What does this mean? Why simply that the soul has assurance, by instincts and presentiments, of *all* power in the direction of its ray, as well as of the special skills it has already acquired.

In order to a knowledge of the resources of the scholar, we must not rest in the use of slender accomplishments, — of faculties to do this and that other feat with words ; but we must pay our vows to the highest power, and pass, if it be possible, by assiduous love and watching, into the visions of absolute truth. The growth of the intellect is strictly analogous in all individuals. It is larger reception. Able men, in general, have good dispositions, and a respect for justice ; because an able man is nothing else than a good, free, vascular organization, whereinto the universal spirit freely flows ; so that his fund of justice is not only vast, but infinite. All men, in the abstract, are just and good ; what hinders them in the particular is the momentary predominance of the finite and individual over the general truth. The condition of our incarnation in a private self seems to be a perpetual tendency to prefer the private law, to obey the private impulse, to the exclusion of the law of universal being. The hero is great by means of the predominance of the universal nature ; he has only to open his mouth, and it speaks ; he has only to be forced to act, and it acts. All men catch the word, or embrace the deed, with the heart, for it is verily theirs as much as his ; but in them this disease of an excess of organization cheats them of equal issues. Nothing is more simple than greatness ; indeed, to be simple is to be great. The vision of genius comes by renouncing the too officious activity of the understanding, and giving leave and amplest privilege to the spontaneous sentiment. Out of this must all that is alive and genial in thought go. Men grind and grind in the mill of a truism, and nothing comes out but what was put in. But the moment they desert the tradition for a spontaneous thought, then poetry, wit, hope, virtue, learning, anecdote, all flock to their aid. Observe the phenomenon of extempore debate. A man of cultivated mind but reserved habits, sitting silent, admires the miracle of free, impassioned, picturesque speech, in the man addressing an assembly; — a state of being and power how unlike his own! Presently his own emotion rises to his lips, and overflows in speech. He must also rise and say somewhat. Once embarked, once having overcome the novelty of the situation, he finds it just as easy and natural to speak, — to speak with thoughts, with pictures, with rhythmical balance of sentences, — as it was to sit silent; for it needs not to do, but to suffer ; he only adjusts himself to the free spirit which gladly utters itself through him ; and motion is as easy as rest.

II. I pass now to consider the task offered to the intellect of this country. The view I have taken of the resources of the scholar, presupposes a subject as broad. We do not seem to have imagined its riches. We have not heeded the invitation it holds out. To be as good a scholar as Englishmen are, to have as much learning as our contemporaries, to have written a book that is read, satisfies us. We assume that all thought is already long ago adequately set down in books, — all imaginations in poems ; and what we say we only throw in as confirmatory of this supposed complete body of literature. A very shallow assumption. Say rather all literature is yet to be written. Poetry has scarce chanted its first song. The perpetual admonition of nature to us, is, ' The world is new, untried. Do not believe the past. I give you the universe a virgin to-day.'

By Latin and English poetry we were born and bred in an oratorio of praises of nature, — flowers, birds, mountains, sun, and moon ; — yet the naturalist of this hour find that he knows nothing, by all their poems, of any of these fine things ; that he has conversed with the mere surface and show of them all ; and of their essence, or of their history, knowing nothing. Further inquiry will discover that nobody, — that not these chanting poets themselves, knew any thing sincere of these handsome natures they so commended ; that they contented themselves with the passing chirp of a bird, that they saw one or two mornings, and listlessly looked at sunsets, and repeated idly these few glimpses in their song. But go into the forest, you shall find all new and undescribed. The honking of the wild geese flying by night; the thin note of the companionable titmouse in the winter day; the fall of swarms of flies, in autumn, from combats high in the air, pattering down on the leaves like rain; the angry hiss of the wood-birds; the pine throwing out its pollen for the benefit of the next century; the turpentine exuding from the tree; — and indeed any vegetation, any animation, any and all, are alike unattempted. The man who stands on the seashore, or who rambles in the woods, seems to be the first man that ever stood on the shore, or entered a grove, his sensations and his world are so novel and strange. Whilst I read the poets, I think that nothing new can be said about morning and evening. But when I see the daybreak I am not reminded of these Homeric, or Shakspearian, or Miltonic, or Chaucerian pictures. No, but I feel perhaps the pain of an alien world; a world not yet subdued by the thought; or I am cheered by the moist, warm, glittering, budding, melodious hour, that takes down the narrow walls of my soul, and extends its life and pulsation to the very horizon. *That* is morning, to cease for a bright hour to be a prisoner of this sickly body, and to become as large as nature.

The noonday darkness of the American forest, the deep, echoing, aboriginal woods, where the living columns of the oak and fir tower up from the ruins of the trees of the last millennium; where, from year to year, the eagle and the crow see no intruder; the pines, bearded with savage moss, yet touched with grace by the violets at their feet; the broad, cold lowland which forms its coat of vapor with the stillness of subterranean crystallization; and where the traveller, amid the repulsive plants that are native in the swamp, thinks with pleasing terror of the distant town; this beauty, — haggard and desert beauty, which the sun and the moon, the snow and the rain, repaint and vary, has never been recorded by art, yet is not indifferent to any passenger. All men are poets at heart. They serve nature for bread, but her loveliness overcomes them sometimes. What mean these journeys to Niagara; these pilgrims to the White Hills? Men believe in the adaptations of utility, always: in the mountains, they may believe in the adaptations of the eye. Undoubtedly the changes of geology have a relation to the prosperous sprouting of the corn and peas in my kitchen garden; but not less is there a relation of beauty between my soul and the dim crags of Agiocochook up there in the clouds. Every man, when this is told, hearkens with joy, and yet his own conversation with nature is still unsung.

Is it otherwise with civil history? Is it not the lesson of our experience that every man, were life long enough, would write history for himself?

What else do these volumes of extracts and manu-
script commentaries, that every scholar writes, indicate ?   Greek history is one thing to me ; another
to you.   Since the birth of Niebuhr and Wolf, Roman and Greek History have been written anew.
Since Carlyle wrote French History, we see that no
history that we have is safe, but a new classifier
shall give it new and more philosophical arrangement.   Thucydides, Livy, have only provided materials.   The moment a man of genius pronounces
the name of the Pelasgi, of Athens, of the Etrurian,
of the Roman people, we see their state under a
new aspect.   As in poetry and history, so in the
other departments.   There are few masters or none.
Religion is yet to be settled on its fast foundations
in the breast of man ; and politics, and philosophy,
and letters, and art.   As yet we have nothing but
tendency and indication.

This starting, this warping of the best literary
works from the adamant of nature, is especially observable in philosophy.   Let it take what tone of
pretension it will, to this complexion must it come,
at last.   Take for example the French Eclecticism,
which Cousin esteems so conclusive ; there is an op-
tical illusion in it.   It avows great pretensions.   It
looks as if they had all truth, in taking all the systems, and had nothing to do but to sift and wash
and strain, and the gold and diamonds would re-

main in the last colander. But, Truth is such a fly-away, such a slyboots, so untransportable and un-barrelable a commodity, that it is as bad to catch as light. Shut the shutters never so quick to keep all the light in, it is all in vain; it is gone before you can cry, Hold. And so it happens with our philosophy. Translate, collate, distil all the systems, it steads you nothing; for truth will not be compelled in any mechanical manner. But the first observation you make, in the sincere act of your nature, though on the veriest trifle, may open a new view of nature and of man, that, like a menstruum, shall dissolve all theories in it; shall take up Greece, Rome, Stoicism, Eclecticism, and what not, as mere data and food for analysis, and dispose of your world-containing system as a very little unit. A profound thought, anywhere, classifies all things : a profound thought will lift Olympus. The book of philosophy is only a fact, and no more inspiring fact than another, and no less; but a wise man will never esteem it anything final and transcending. Go and talk with a man of genius, and the first word he utters, sets all your so-called knowledge afloat and at large. Then Plato, Bacon, Kant, and the Eclectic Cousin condescend instantly to be men and mere facts.

I by no means aim in these remarks to disparage the merit of these or of any existing compositions ;

I only say that any particular portraiture does not in any manner exclude or forestall a new attempt, but, when considered by the soul, warps and shrinks away. The inundation of the spirit sweeps away before it all our little architecture of wit and memory, as straws and straw-huts before the torrent. Works of the intellect are great only by comparison with each other; Ivanhoe and Waverley compared with Castle Radcliffe and the Porter novels; but nothing is great, — not mighty Homer and Milton, — beside the infinite Reason. It carries them away as a flood. They are as a sleep.

Thus is justice done to each generation and individual, — wisdom teaching man that he shall not hate, or fear, or mimic his ancestors; that he shall not bewail himself, as if the world was old, and thought was spent, and he was born into the dotage of things; for, by virtue of the Deity, thought renews itself inexhaustibly every day, and the thing whereon it shines, though it were dust and sand, is a new subject with countless relations.

III. Having thus spoken of the resources and the subject of the scholar, out of the same faith proceeds also the rule of his ambition and life. Let him know that the world is his, but he must possess it by putting himself into harmony with the

constitution of things.   He must be a solitary, laborious, modest, and charitable soul.

He must embrace solitude as a bride.   He must
have his glees and his glooms alone.   His own estimate must be measure enough, his own praise reward enough for him.   And why must the student
be solitary and silent?   That he may become acquainted with his thoughts.   If he pines in a lonely
place, hankering for the crowd, for display, he is
not in the lonely place ; his heart is in the market ;
he does not see ; he does not hear ; he does not
think.   But go cherish your soul ; expel companions ; set your habits to a life of solitude ; then will
the faculties rise fair and full within, like forest
trees and field flowers ; you will have results,
which, when you meet your fellow-men, you can
communicate, and they will gladly receive.   Do not
go into solitude only that you may presently come
into public.   Such solitude denies itself ; is public
and stale.   The public can get public experience,
but they wish the scholar to replace to them those
private, sincere, divine experiences of which they
have been defrauded by dwelling in the street.   It
is the noble, manlike, just thought, which is the
superiority demanded of you, and not crowds but
solitude confers this elevation.   Not insulation of
place, but independence of spirit is essential, and
it is only as the garden, the cottage, the forest, and

the rock, are a sort of mechanical aids to this, that
they are of value. Think alone, and all places are
friendly and sacred. The poets who have lived in
cities have been hermits still. Inspiration makes
solitude anywhere. Pindar, Raphael, Angelo,
Dryden, De Staël, dwell in crowds it may be, but
the instant thought comes the crowd grows dim to
their eye; their eye fixes on the horizon, on va-
cant space; they forget the by-standers; they spurn
personal relations; they deal with abstractions,
with verities, with ideas. They are alone with the
mind.

Of course I would not have any superstition
about solitude. Let the youth study the uses of
solitude and of society. Let him use both, not
serve either. The reason why an ingenious soul
shuns society, is to the end of finding society.
It repudiates the false, out of love of the true.
You can very soon learn all that society can teach
you for one while. Its foolish routine, an indefinite multiplication of balls, concerts, rides, theatres,
can teach you no more than a few can. Then accept the hint of shame, of spiritual emptiness and
waste which true nature gives you, and retire and
hide; lock the door; shut the shutters; then welcome falls the imprisoning rain, — dear hermitage
of nature. Re-collect the spirits. Have solitary
prayer and praise. Digest and correct the past

experience ; and blend it with the new and divine life.

You will pardon me, Gentlemen, if I say I think that we have need of a more rigorous scholastic rule ; such an asceticism, I mean, as only the hardihood and devotion of the scholar himself can enforce. We live in the sun and on the surface, — a thin, plausible, superficial existence, and talk of muse and prophet, of art and creation. But out of our shallow and frivolous way of life, how can greatness ever grow ? Come now, let us go and be dumb. Let us sit with our hands on our mouths, a long, austere, Pythagorean lustrum. Let us live in corners, and do chores, and suffer, and weep, and drudge, with eyes and hearts that love the Lord. Silence, seclusion, austerity, may pierce deep into the grandeur and secret of our being, and so diving, bring up out of secular darkness the sublimities of the moral constitution. How mean to go blazing, a gaudy butterfly, in fashionable or political saloons, the fool of society, the fool of notoriety, a topic for newspapers, a piece of the street, and forfeiting the real prerogative of the russet coat, the privacy, and the true and warm heart of the citizen !

Fatal to the man of letters, fatal to man, is the lust of display, the seeming that unmakes our being. A mistake of the main end to which they

labor is incident to literary men, who, dealing with
the organ of language, — the subtlest, strongest,
and longest-lived of man's creations, and only fitly
used as the weapon of thought and of justice, —
learn to enjoy the pride of playing with this splendid engine, but rob it of its almightiness by failing
to work with it. Extricating themselves from the
tasks of the world, the world revenges itself by
exposing, at every turn, the folly of these incom-
plete, pedantic, useless, ghostly creatures. The
scholar will feel that the richest romance, the
noblest fiction that was ever woven, the heart and
soul of beauty, lies enclosed in human life. Itself of surpassing value, it is also the richest material for his creations. How shall he know its secrets of tenderness, of terror, of will, and of fate?
How can he catch and keep the strain of upper
music that peals from it? Its laws are concealed
under the details of daily action. All action is an
experiment upon them. He must bear his share
of the common load. He must work with men in
houses, and not with their names in books. His
needs, appetites, talents, affections, accomplishments, are keys that open to him the beautiful
museum of human life. Why should he read it as
an Arabian tale, and not know, in his own beating
bosom, its sweet and smart? Out of love and
hatred, out of earnings, and borrowings, and lend-

ings, and losses; out of sickness and pain; out of wooing and worshipping; out of travelling, and voting, and watching, and caring; out of disgrace and contempt, comes our tuition in the serene and beautiful laws. Let him not slur his lesson; let him learn it by heart. Let him endeavor exactly, bravely, and cheerfully, to solve the problem of that life which is set before *him*. And this by punctual action, and not by promises or dreams. Believing, as in God, in the presence and favor of the grandest influences, let him deserve that favor, and learn how to receive and use it, by fidelity also to the lower observances.

This lesson is taught with emphasis in the life of the great actor of this age, and affords the explanation of his success. Bonaparte represents truly a great recent revolution, which we in this country, please God, shall carry to its farthest consummation. Not the least instructive passage in modern history seems to me a trait of Napoleon exhibited to the English when he became their prisoner. On coming on board the Bellerophon, a file of English soldiers drawn up on deck gave him a military salute. Napoleon observed that their manner of handling their arms differed from the French exercise, and, putting aside the guns of those nearest him, walked up to a soldier, took his gun, and himself went through the motion in the French mode. The English officers and men looked on with astonishment, and inquired if such familiarity was usual with the Emperor.

In this instance, as always, that man, with whatever defects or vices, represented performance in lieu of pretension. Feudalism and Orientalism had long enough thought it majestic to do nothing; the modern majesty consists in work. He belonged to a class fast growing in the world, who think that what a man can do is his greatest ornament, and that he always consults his dignity by doing it. He was not a believer in luck; he had a faith, like sight, in the application of means to ends. Means to ends, is the motto of all his behavior. He believed that the great captains of antiquity performed their exploits only by correct combinations, and by justly comparing the relation between means and consequences, efforts and obstacles. The vulgar call good fortune that which really is produced by the calculations of genius. But Napoleon, thus faithful to facts, had also this crowning merit, that whilst he believed in number and weight, and omitted no part of prudence, he believed also in the freedom and quite incalculable force of the soul. A man of infinite caution, he neglected never the least particular of preparation, of patient adaptation; yet nevertheless he had a sublime confidence, as in his all, in the sallies of the courage, and the faith in his destiny, which, at the right moment, repaired all losses, and demolished cavalry, infantry, king, and kaisar, as with irresistible thunderbolts. As they say the bough of the tree has the character of the leaf, and the whole tree of the bough, so, it is curious to remark, Bonaparte's army partook of this double strength of the captain; for, whilst strictly supplied in all its appointments, and everything expected from the valor and discipline of every platoon, in flank and centre, yet always remained his total trust in the prodigious revolutions of fortune which his reserved Imperial Guard were capable of working, if, in all else, the day was lost. Here he was sublime. He no longer calculated the chance of the cannon ball. He was faithful to tactics to the uttermost, — and when all tactics had come to an end then he dilated and availed himself of the mighty saltations of the most formidable soldiers in nature.

Let the scholar appreciate this combination of gifts, which, applied to better purpose, make true wisdom. He is a revealer of things. Let him first learn the things. Let him not, too eager to grasp some badge of reward, omit the work to be done. Let him know that though the success of the market is in the reward, true success is the doing; that, in the private obedience to his mind; in the sedulous inquiry, day after day, year after year, to know how the thing stands; in the use of all means, and most in the reverence of the humble commerce and humble needs of life, — to hearken what *they* say, and so, by mutual reaction of thought and life, to make thought solid, and life wise; and in a contempt for the gabble of to-day's opinions the secret of the world is to be learned, and the skill truly to unfold it is acquired. Or, rather, is it not, that, by this discipline, the usurpation of the senses is overcome, and the lower faculties of man are subdued to docility; through which as an unobstructed channel the soul now easily and gladly flows?

The good scholar will not refuse to bear the yoke in his youth; to know, if he can, the uttermost secret of toil and endurance; to make his own hands acquainted with the soil by which he is fed, and the sweat that goes before comfort and luxury. Let him pay his tithe and serve the world as a true and noble man; never forgetting to worship the immortal divinities who whisper to the poet and make him the utterer of melodies that pierce the ear of eternal time. If he have this twofold goodness, — the drill and the inspiration, — then he has health; then he is a whole, and not a fragment; and the perfection of his endowment will appear in his compositions. Indeed, this twofold merit character-

izes ever the productions of great masters. The
man of genius should occupy the whole space between God or pure mind and the multitude of un-
educated men. He must draw from the infinite
Reason, on one side; and he must penetrate into
the heart and sense of the crowd, on the other.
From one, he must draw his strength; to the other,
he must owe his aim. The one yokes him to the
real; the other, to the apparent. At one pole is
Reason; at the other, Common Sense. If he be
defective at either extreme of the scale, his philosophy will seem low and utilitarian, or it will appear
too vague and indefinite for the uses of life.

The student, as we all along insist, is great only
by being passive to the superincumbent spirit. Let
this faith then dictate all his action. Snares and
bribes abound to mislead him; let him be true
nevertheless. His success has its perils too. There
is somewhat inconvenient and injurious in his position. They whom his thoughts have entertained or
inflamed, seek him before yet they have learned
the hard conditions of thought. They seek him,
that he may turn his lamp on the dark riddles
whose solution they think is inscribed on the walls
of their being. They find that he is a poor, ignorant man, in a white-seamed, rusty coat, like themselves, nowise emitting a continuous stream of
light, but now and then a jet of luminous thought

followed by total darkness; moreover, that he cannot make of his infrequent illumination a portable
taper to carry whither he would, and explain now
this dark riddle, now that. Sorrow ensues. The
scholar regrets to damp the hope of ingenuous
boys; and the youth has lost a star out of his new
flaming firmament. Hence the temptation to the
scholar to mystify, to hear the question, to sit upon
it, to make an answer of words in lack of the oracle
of things. Not the less let him be cold and true,
and wait in patience, knowing that truth can make
even silence eloquent and memorable. Truth shall
be policy enough for him. Let him open his
breast to all honest inquiry, and be an artist superior to tricks of art. Show frankly as a saint would
do, your experience, methods, tools, and means.
Welcome all comers to the freest use of the same.
And out of this superior frankness and charity
you shall learn higher secrets of your nature,
which gods will bend and aid you to communicate.

If, with a high trust, he can thus submit himself,
he will find that ample returns are poured into his
bosom out of what seemed hours of obstruction
and loss. Let him not grieve too much on account
of unfit associates. When he sees how much
thought he owes to the disagreeable antagonism
of various persons who pass and cross him, he can
easily think that in a society of perfect sympathy,

no word, no act, no record, would be. He will
learn that it is not much matter what he reads,
what he does. Be a scholar, and he shall have the
scholar's part of everything. As in the counting-
room the merchant cares little whether the cargo
be hides or barilla; the transaction, a letter of
credit or a transfer of stocks; be it what it may,
his commission comes gently out of it; so you shall
get your lesson out of the hour, and the object,
whether it be a concentrated or a wasteful employment, even in reading a dull book, or working off
a stint of mechanical day-labor which your necessities or the necessities of others impose.

Gentlemen, I have ventured to offer you these
considerations upon the scholar's place and hope,
because I thought that standing, as many of you
now do, on the threshold of this College, girt and
ready to go and assume tasks, public and private,
in your country, you would not be sorry to be ad-
monished of those primary duties of the intellect
whereof you will seldom hear from the lips of your
new companions. You will hear every day the
maxims of a low prudence. You will hear that
the first duty is to get land and money, place and
name. 'What is this Truth you seek? what is
this Beauty?' men will ask, with derision. If
nevertheless God have called any of you to explore

truth and beauty, be bold, be firm, be true. When you shall say, 'As others do, so will I : I renounce, I am sorry for it, my early visions ; I must eat the good of the land and let learning and romantic expectations go, until a more convenient season ; ' — then dies the man in you ; then once more perish the buds of art, and poetry, and science, as they have died already in a thousand thousand men. The hour of that choice is the crisis of your history, and see that you hold yourself fast by the intellect. It is this domineering temper of the sensual world that creates the extreme need of the priests of science ; and it is the office and right of the intellect to make and not take its estimate. Bend to the persuasion which is flowing to you from every object in nature, to be its tongue to the heart of man, and to show the besotted world how passing fair is wisdom. Forewarned that the vice of the times and the country is an excessive pretension, let us seek the shade, and find wisdom in neglect. Be content with a little light, so it be your own. Explore, and explore. Be neither chided nor flattered out of your position of perpetual inquiry. Neither dogmatize, nor accept another's dogmatism. Why should you renounce your right to traverse the star-lit deserts of truth, for the premature comforts of an acre, house, and barn? Truth also has its roof, and bed, and board.

Make yourself necessary to the world, and mankind will give you bread, and if not store of it, yet such as shall not take away your property in all men's possessions, in all men's affections, in art, in nature, and in hope.

You will not fear that I am enjoining too stern an asceticism. Ask not, Of what use is a scholarship that systematically retreats? or, Who is the better for the philosopher who conceals his accomplishments, and hides his thoughts from the waiting world? Hides his thoughts! Hide the sun and moon. Thought is all light, and publishes itself to the universe. It will speak, though you were dumb, by its own miraculous organ. It will flow out of your actions, your manners, and your face. It will bring you friendships. It will impledge you to truth by the love and expectation of generous minds. By virtue of the laws of that Nature which is one and perfect, it shall yield every sincere good that is in the soul to the scholar beloved of earth and heaven.

THE METHOD OF NATURE.

AN ORATION DELIVERED BEFORE THE SOCIETY OF THE ADELPHI,
IN WATERVILLE COLLEGE, MAINE, AUGUST 11, 1841.

THE METHOD OF NATURE.

———◆———

GENTLEMEN,

Let us exchange congratulations on the enjoyments and the promises of this literary anniversary. The land we live in has no interest so dear, if it knew its want, as the fit consecration of days of reason and thought. Where there is no vision, the people perish. The scholars are the priests of that thought which establishes the foundations of the earth. No matter what is their special work or profession, they stand for the spiritual interest of the world, and it is a common calamity if they neglect their post in a country where the material interest is so predominant as it is in America. We hear something too much of the results of machinery, commerce, and the useful arts. We are a puny and a fickle folk. Avarice, hesitation, and following, are our diseases. The rapid wealth which hundreds in the community acquire in trade, or by the incessant expansions of our population and arts, enchants the eyes of all the rest; the luck of one is the hope of thousands, and the bribe acts like the neighborhood of a gold mine to impoverish the farm, the school, the church, the house, and the very body and feature of man.

I do not wish to look with sour aspect at the industrious manufacturing village, or the mart of commerce. I love the music of the water-wheel; I value the railway; I feel the pride which the sight of a ship inspires; I look on trade and every mechanical craft as education also. But let me discriminate what is precious herein. There is in each of these works an act of invention, an intellectual step, or short series of steps, taken; that act or step is the spiritual act; all the rest is mere repetition of the same a thousand times. And I will not be deceived into admiring the routine of handicrafts and mechanics, how splendid soever the result, any more than I admire the routine of the scholars or clerical class. That splendid results ensue from the labors of stupid men, is the fruit of higher laws than their will, and the routine is not to be praised for it. I would not have the laborer sacrificed to the result, — I would not have the laborer sacrificed to my convenience and pride, nor to that of a great class of such as me. Let there be worse cotton and better men. The weaver should not be bereaved of his superiority to his work, and his knowledge that the product or the skill is of no value, except so far as it embodies his spiritual prerogatives. If I see nothing to admire in the unit, shall I admire a million units? Men stand in awe of the city, but do not honor any individual citizen; and are continually yielding to this dazzling result of numbers, that which they would never yield to the solitary example of any one.

Whilst the multitude of men degrade each other, and give currency to desponding doctrines, the scholar must be a bringer of hope, and must reinforce man against himself. I sometimes believe that our literary anniversaries will presently assume a greater importance, as the eyes of men open to their capabilities. Here, a new set of distinctions, a new order of ideas, prevail. Here, we set a bound to the respectability of wealth, and a bound to the pretensions of the law and the church. The bigot must cease to be a bigot to-day. Into our charmed circle, power cannot enter; and the sturdiest defender of existing institutions feels the terrific inflammability of this air which condenses heat in every corner that may restore to the elements the fabrics of ages. Nothing solid is secure; every thing tilts and rocks. Even the scholar is not safe; he too is searched and revised. Is his learning dead? Is he living in his memory? The power of mind is not mortification, but life. But come forth, thou curious child! hither, thou loving, all-hoping poet! hither, thou tender, doubting heart,

which hast not yet found any place in the world's
market fit for thee; any wares which thou couldst
buy or sell, — so large is thy love and ambition, —
thine and not theirs is the hour. Smooth thy brow,
and hope and love on, for the kind Heaven justifies
thee, and the whole world feels that thou art in the
right.

We ought to celebrate this hour by expressions
of manly joy. Not thanks, not prayer seem quite
the highest or truest name for our communication
with the infinite, — but glad and conspiring reception, — reception that becomes giving in its turn,
as the receiver is only the All-Giver in part and in
infancy. I cannot, — nor can any man, — speak precisely of things so sublime, but it seems to me the
wit of man, his strength, his grace, his tendency,
his art, is the grace and the presence of God. It is
beyond explanation. When all is said and done,
the rapt saint is found the only logician. Not
exhortation, not argument becomes our lips, but
pæans of joy and praise. But not of adulation:
we are too nearly related in the deep of the mind
to that we honor. It is God in us which checks the
language of petition by a grander thought. In the
bottom of the heart it is said; 'I am, and by me,
O child! this fair body and world of thine stands
and grows. I am; all things are mine: and all
mine are thine.'

The festival of the intellect and the return to its source cast a strong light on the always interesting topics of Man and Nature. We are forcibly reminded of the old want. There is no man ; there hath never been. The Intellect still asks that a man may be born. The flame of life flickers feebly in human breasts. We demand of men a richness and universality we do not find. Great men do not content us. It is their solitude, not their force, that makes them conspicuous. There is somewhat indigent and tedious about them. They are poorly tied to one thought. If they are prophets they are egotists ; if polite and various they are shallow. How tardily men arrive at any result! how tardily they pass from it to another! The crystal sphere of thought is as concentrical as the geological structure of the globe. As our soils and rocks lie in strata, concentric strata, so do all men's thinkings run laterally, never vertically. Here comes by a great inquisitor with auger and plumb-line, and will bore an Artesian well through our conventions and theories, and pierce to the core of things. But as soon as he probes the crust, behold gimlet, plumb-line, and philosopher take a lateral direction, in spite of all resistance, as if some strong wind took everything off its feet, and if you come month after month to see what progress our reformer has made, — not an inch has he pierced, —

you still find him with new words in the old place, floating about in new parts of the same old vein or crust. The new book says, ' I will give you the key to nature,' and we expect to go like a thunder-bolt to the centre. But the thunder is a surface phenomenon, makes a skin-deep cut, and so does the sage. The wedge turns out to be a rocket. Thus a man lasts but a very little while, for his monomania becomes insupportably tedious in a few months. It is so with every book and person : and yet — and yet — we do not take up a new book or meet a new man without a pulse-beat of expecta-tion. And this invincible hope of a more adequate interpreter is the sure prediction of his advent.

In the absence of man, we turn to nature, which stands next. In the divine order, intellect is pri-mary ; nature, secondary ; it is the memory of the mind. That which once existed in intellect as pure law, has now taken body as Nature. It existed al-ready in the mind in solution ; now, it has been precipitated, and the bright sediment is the world. We can never be quite strangers or inferiors in na-ture. It is flesh of our flesh, and bone of our bone. But we no longer hold it by the hand ; we have lost our miraculous power ; our arm is no more as strong as the frost, nor our will equivalent to gravity and the elective attractions. Yet we can use nature as a convenient standard, and the meter of our rise and fall. It has this advantage as a witness, it cannot be debauched. When man curses, nature still testifies to truth and love. We may therefore safely study the mind in nature, because we cannot steadily gaze on it in mind ; as we explore the face of the sun in a pool, when our eyes cannot brook his direct splendors.

It seems to me therefore that it were some suitable pæan if we should piously celebrate this hour by exploring the *method of nature.* Let us see *that,* as nearly as we can, and try how far it is transferable to the literary life. Every earnest glance we give to the realities around us, with intent to learn, proceeds from a holy impulse, and is really songs of praise. What difference can it make whether it take the shape of exhortation, or of passionate exclamation, or of scientific statement ? These are forms merely. Through them we express, at last, the fact that God has done thus or thus.

In treating a subject so large, in which we must necessarily appeal to the intuition, and aim much more to suggest than to describe, I know it is not easy to speak with the precision attainable on topics of less scope. I do not wish in attempting to paint a man, to describe an air-fed, unimpassioned, impossible ghost. My eyes and ears are revolted by any neglect of the physical facts, the limitations of man. And yet one who conceives the true order of nature, and beholds the visible as proceeding from the invisible, cannot state his thought without seeming to those who study the physical laws to do them some injustice. There is an intrinsic defect in the organ. Language overstates. Statements of the infinite are usually felt to be unjust to the finite, and blasphemous. Empedocles undoubtedly spoke a truth of thought, when he said, " I am God ; " but the moment it was out of his mouth it became a lie to the ear; and the world revenged itself for the seeming arrogance by the good story about his shoe. How can I hope for better hap in my attempts to enunciate spiritual facts ? Yet let us hope that as far as we receive the truth, so far shall we be felt by every true person to say what is just.

The method of nature : who could ever analyze it ? That rushing stream will not stop to be observed. We can never surprise nature in a corner ; never find the end of a thread ; never tell where to set the first stone. The bird hastens to lay her egg : the egg hastens to be a bird. The wholeness we admire in the order of the world is the result of infinite distribution. Its smoothness is the smoothness of the pitch of the cataract. Its permanence is a perpetual inchoation. Every natural fact is an emanation, and that from which it emanates is an emanation also, and from every emanation is a new emanation. If anything could stand still, it would be crushed and dissipated by the torrent it resisted, and if it were a mind, would be crazed ; as insane persons are those who hold fast to one thought and do not flow with the course of nature. Not the cause, but an ever novel effect, nature descends always from above. It is unbroken obedience. The beauty of these fair objects is imported into them from a metaphysical and eternal spring. In all animal and vegetable forms, the physiologist concedes that no chemistry, no mechanics, can account for the facts, but a mysterious principle of life must be assumed, which not only inhabits the organ but makes the organ.

How silent, how spacious, what room for all, yet without place to insert an atom ; — in graceful succession, in equal fulness, in balanced beauty, the dance of the hours goes forward still. Like an odor of incense, like a strain of music, like a sleep, it is inexact and boundless. It will not be dissected, nor unravelled, nor shown. Away profane philosopher! seekest thou in nature the cause? This refers to that, and that to the next, and the next to the third, and everything refers. Thou must ask in another mood, thou must feel it and love it, thou must behold it in a spirit as grand as that by which it exists, ere thou canst know the law.   Known it will not be, but gladly beloved and enjoyed.

The simultaneous life throughout the whole body, the equal serving of innumerable ends without the least emphasis or preference to any, but the steady degradation of each to the success of all, allows the understanding no place to work.   Nature can only be conceived as existing to a universal and not to a particular end; to a universe of ends, and not to one, — a work of *ecstasy*, to be represented by a circular movement, as intention might be signified by a straight line of definite length.   Each effect strengthens every other.   There is no revolt in all the kingdoms from the commonweal : no detachment of an individual.   Hence the catholic character which makes every leaf an exponent of the world.   When we behold the landscape in a poetic spirit, we do not reckon individuals.   Nature knows neither palm nor oak, but only vegetable life, which sprouts into forests, and festoons the globe with a garland of grasses and vines.

That no single end may be selected and nature judged thereby, appears from this, that if man himself be considered as the end, and it be assumed that the final cause of the world is to make holy or wise or beautiful men, we see that it has not succeeded.   Read alternately in natural and in civil history, a treatise of astronomy, for example, with a volume of French *Mémoires pour servir.* When we have spent our wonder in computing this wasteful hospitality with which boon Nature turns off new firmaments without end into her wide common, as fast as the madrepores make coral, — suns and planets hospitable to souls, — and then shorten the sight to look into this court of Louis Quatorze, and see the game that is played there, — duke and marshal, abbé and madame, — a gambling table where each is laying traps for the other, where the end is ever by some lie or fetch to outwit your rival and ruin him with this solemn fop in wig and stars, — the king; — one can hardly help asking if this planet is a fair specimen of the so generous astronomy, and if so, whether the experiment have not failed, and whether it be quite worth while to make more, and glut the innocent space with so poor an article.

I think we feel not much otherwise if, instead of beholding foolish nations, we take the great and wise men, the eminent souls, and narrowly inspect their biography. None of them seen by himself, and his performance compared with his promise or idea, will justify the cost of that enormous apparatus of means by which this spotted and defective person was at last procured.

To questions of this sort, Nature replies, "I grow." All is nascent, infant. When we are dizzied with

the arithmetic of the savant toiling to compute the
length of her line, the return of her curve, we are
steadied by the perception that a great deal is doing;
that all seems just begun : remote aims are in active accomplishment.   We can point nowhere to
anything final; but tendency appears on all hands :
planet, system, constellation, total nature is growing like a field of maize in July; is becoming somewhat else ; is in rapid metamorphosis.   The embryo
does not more strive to be man, than yonder burr
of light we call a nebula tends to be a ring, a com-
et, a globe, and parent of new stars.   Why should
not then these messieurs of Versailles strut and
plot for tabourets and ribbons, for a season, without prejudice to their faculty to run on better
errands by and by?

But Nature seems further to reply, ' I have ventured so great a stake as my success, in no single
creature.   I have not yet arrived at any end.   The
gardener aims to produce a fine peach or pear, but
my aim is the health of the whole tree, — root,
stem, leaf, flower, and seed, — and by no means
the pampering of a monstrous pericarp at the expense of all the other functions.'

In short, the spirit and peculiarity of that impression nature makes on us is this, that it does
not exist to any one or to any number of particular
ends, but to numberless and endless benefit; that

there is in it no private will, no rebel leaf or limb, but the whole is oppressed by one superincumbent tendency, obeys that redundancy or excess of life which in conscious beings we call *ecstasy.*

With this conception of the genius or method of nature, let us go back to man. It is true he pretends to give account of himself to himself, but, at last, what has he to recite but the fact that there is a Life not to be described or known otherwise than by possession? What account can he give of his essence more than *so it was to be?* The *royal* reason, the Grace of God, seems the only description of our multiform but ever identical fact. There is virtue, there is genius, there is success, or there is not. There is the incoming or the receding of God: that is all we can affirm; and we can show neither how nor why. Self-accusation, remorse, and the didactic morals of self-denial and strife with sin, is a view we are constrained by our constitution to take of the fact seen from the platform of action; but seen from the platform of intellection there is nothing for us but praise and wonder.

The termination of the world in a man appears to be the last victory of intelligence. The universal does not attract us until housed in an individual. Who heeds the waste abyss of possibility? The ocean is everywhere the same, but it has no character until seen with the shore or the ship.

Who would value any number of miles of Atlantic brine bounded by lines of latitude and longitude? Confine it by granite rocks, let it wash a shore where wise men dwell, and it is filled with expression ; and the point of greatest interest is where the land and water meet. So must we admire in man the form of the formless, the concentration of the vast, the house of reason, the cave of memory. See the play of thoughts! what nimble gigantic creatures are these! what saurians, what palaiotheria shall be named with these agile movers? The great Pan of old, who was clothed in a leopard skin to signify the beautiful variety of things and the firmament, his coat of stars, — was but the representative of thee, O rich and various Man! thou palace of sight and sound, carrying in thy senses the morning and the night and the unfathomable galaxy ; in thy brain, the geometry of the City of God ; in thy heart, the bower of love and the realms of right and wrong. An individual man is a fruit which it cost all the foregoing ages to form and ripen. The history of the genesis or the old mythology repeats itself in the experience of every child. He too is a demon or god thrown into a particular chaos, where he strives ever to lead things from disorder into order. Each individual soul is such in virtue of its being a power to translate the world into some particular language of its own; if not into a picture, a statue, or a dance, — why, then, into a trade, an art, a science, a mode of living, a conversation, a character, an influence. You admire pictures, but it is as impossible for you to paint a right picture as for grass to bear apples. But when the genius comes, it makes fingers: it is pliancy, and the power of transferring the affair in the street into oils and colors. Raphael must be born, and Salvator must be born.

There is no attractiveness like that of a new man. The sleepy nations are occupied with their political routine. England, France and America read Parliamentary Debates, which no high genius now enlivens; and nobody will read them who trusts his own eye: only they who are deceived by the popular repetition of distinguished names. But when Napoleon unrolls his map, the eye is commanded by original power. When Chatham leads the debate, men may well listen, because they must listen. A man, a personal ascendency, is the only great phenomenon. When Nature has work to be done, she creates a genius to do it. Follow the great man, and you shall see what the world has at heart in these ages. There is no omen like that.

But what strikes us in the fine genius is that which belongs of right to every one. A man should know himself for a necessary actor. A link was wanting between two craving parts of nature, and he was hurled into being as the bridge over that yawning need, the mediator betwixt two else unmarriageable facts. His two parents held each of one of the wants, and the union of foreign constitutions in him enables him to do gladly and gracefully what the assembled human race could not have sufficed to do. He knows his materials ; he applies himself to his work ; he cannot read, or think, or look, but he unites the hitherto separated strands into a perfect cord. The thoughts he delights to utter are the reason of his incarnation. Is it for him to account himself cheap and superfluous, or to linger by the wayside for opportunities? Did he not come into being because something must be done which he and no other is and does? If only he *sees*, the world will be visible enough. He need not study where to stand, nor to put things in favorable lights ; in him is the light, from him all things are illuminated to their centre. What patron shall he ask for employment and reward? Hereto was he born, to deliver the thought of his heart from the universe to the universe ; to do an office which nature could not forego, nor he be discharged from rendering, and then immerge again into the holy silence and eternity out of which as a man he arose. God is rich, and many more men than one he harbors in his bosom, biding their time and the needs and the beauty of all. Is not this the theory of every man's genius or faculty? Why then goest thou as some Boswell or listening worshipper to this saint or to that? That is the only lese-majesty. Here art thou with whom so long the universe travailed in labor; darest thou think meanly of thyself whom the stalwart Fate brought forth to unite his ragged sides, to shoot the gulf, to reconcile the irreconcilable?

Whilst a necessity so great caused the man to exist, his health and erectness consist in the fidelity with which he transmits influences from the vast and universal to the point on which his genius can act. The ends are momentary; they are vents for the current of inward life which increases as it is spent. A man's wisdom is to know that all ends are momentary, that the best end must be superseded by a better. But there is a mischievous tendency in him to transfer his thought from the life to the ends, to quit his agency and rest in his acts: the tools run away with the workman, the human with the divine. I conceive a man as always spoken to from behind, and unable to turn his head and see the speaker. In all the millions who have heard the voice, none ever saw the face. As children in their play run behind each other, and seize one by the ears and make him walk before them, so is the spirit our unseen pilot. That well-known voice speaks in all languages, governs all men, and none ever caught a glimpse of its form. If the man will exactly obey it, it will adopt him, so that he shall not any longer separate it from himself in his thought; he shall seem to be it, he shall be it. If he listen with insatiable ears, richer and greater wisdom is taught him; the sound swells to a ravishing music, he is borne away as with a flood, he becomes careless of his food and of his house, he is the fool of ideas, and leads a heavenly life. But if his eye is set on the things to be done, and not on the truth that is still taught, and for the sake of which the things are to be done, then the voice grows faint, and at last is but a humming in his ears. His health and greatness consist in his being the channel through which heaven flows to earth, in short, in the fulness in which an ecstatical state takes place in him. It is pitiful to be an artist, when by forbearing to be artists we might be vessels filled with the divine overflowings, enriched by the circulations of omniscience and omnipresence. Are there not moments in the history of heaven when the human race was not counted by individuals, but was only the Influenced, was God in distribution, God rushing into multiform benefit? It is sublime to receive, sublime to love, but this lust of imparting as from *us*, this desire to be loved, the wish to be recognized as individuals, — is finite, comes of a lower strain.

Shall I say then that as far as we can trace the natural history of the soul, its health consists in the fulness of its reception? — call it piety, call it veneration, — in the fact that enthusiasm is organized therein. What is best in any work of art but that part which the work itself seems to require and do; that which the man cannot do again; that which flows from the hour and the occasion, like the eloquence of men in a tumultuous debate? It was always the theory of literature that the word of a poet was authoritative and final. He was supposed to be the mouth of a divine wisdom. We rather envied his circumstance than his talent. We too could have gladly prophesied standing in that place. We so quote our Scriptures; and the Greeks so quoted Homer, Theognis, Pindar, and the rest. If the theory has receded out of modern criticism, it is because we have not had poets. Whenever they appear, they will redeem their own credit.

This ecstatical state seems to direct a regard to the whole and not to the parts; to the cause and not to the ends; to the tendency and not to the act. It respects genius and not talent; hope, and not possession; the anticipation of all things by the intellect, and not the history itself; art, and not works of art; poetry, and not experiment; virtue, and not duties.

There is no office or function of man but is rightly discharged by this divine method, and nothing that is not noxious to him if detached from its universal relations. Is it his work in the world to study nature, or the laws of the world? Let him beware of proposing to himself any end. Is it for use? nature is debased, as if one looking at the ocean can remember only the price of fish. Or is it for pleasure? he is mocked; there is a certain infatuating air in woods and mountains which draws on the idler to want and misery. There is something social and intrusive in the nature of all things; they seek to penetrate and overpower each the nature of every other creature, and itself alone in all modes and throughout space and spirit to prevail and possess. Every star in heaven is discontented and insatiable. Gravitation and chemistry cannot content them. Ever they woo and court the eye of every beholder. Every man who comes into the world they seek to fascinate and possess, to pass into his mind, for they desire to republish themselves in a more delicate world than that they occupy. It is not enough that they are Jove, Mars, Orion, and the North Star, in the gravitating firmament; they would have such poets as Newton, Herschel, and Laplace, that they may re-exist and re-appear in the finer world of rational souls, and fill that realm with their fame. So is it with all immaterial objects. These beautiful basilisks set their brute glorious eyes on the eye of every child, and, if they can, cause their nature to pass through his wondering eyes into him, and so all things are mixed.

Therefore man must be on his guard against this cup of enchantments, and must look at nature with a supernatural eye. By piety alone, by conversing with the cause of nature, is he safe and commands it. And because all knowledge is assimilation to the object of knowledge, as the power or genius of nature is ecstatic, so must its science or the description of it be. The poet must be a rhapsodist; his inspiration a sort of bright casualty; his will in it only the surrender of will to the Universal Power, which will not be seen face to face, but must be received and sympathetically known. It is remarkable that we have out of the deeps of antiquity in the oracles ascribed to the half fabulous Zoroaster, a statement of this fact which every lover and seeker of truth will recognize. "It is not proper," said Zoroaster, " to understand the Intelligible with vehemence, but if you incline your mind, you will apprehend it: not too earnestly, but bringing a pure and inquiring eye. You will not understand it as when understanding some particular thing, but with the flower of the mind. Things divine are not attainable by mortals who understand sensual things, but only the light-armed arrive at the summit."

And because ecstasy is the law and cause of nature, therefore you cannot interpret it in too high and deep a sense. Nature represents the best meaning of the wisest man. Does the sunset landscape seem to you the place of Friendship, — those purple skies and lovely waters the amphitheatre dressed and garnished only for the exchange of thought and love of the purest souls? It is that. All other meanings which base men have put on it are conjectural and false. You cannot bathe twice in the same river, said Heraclitus; and I add, a man never sees the same object twice: with his own enlargement the object acquires new aspects.

Does not the same law hold for virtue? It is vitiated by too much will. He who aims at progress should aim at an infinite, not at a special benefit. The reforms whose fame now fills the land with Temperance, Anti-Slavery, Non-Resistance, No Government, Equal Labor, fair and generous as each appears, are poor bitter things when prosecuted for themselves as an end. To every reform, in proportion to its energy, early disgusts are incident, so that the disciple is surprised at the very hour of his first triumphs with chagrins; and sickness, and a general distrust; so that he shuns his associates, hates the enterprise which lately seemed

so fair, and meditates to cast himself into the arms
of that society and manner of life which he had
newly abandoned with so much pride and hope.
Is it that he attached the value of virtue to some
particular practices, as the denial of certain appetites in certain specified indulgences, and afterward
found himself still as wicked and as far from happiness in that abstinence as he had been in the
abuse? But the soul can be appeased not by a
deed but by a tendency. It is in a hope that she
feels her wings. You shall love rectitude, and not
the disuse of money or the avoidance of trade; an
unimpeded mind, and not a monkish diet; sympathy and usefulness, and not hoeing or coopering.
Tell me not how great your project is, the civil lib-
eration of the world, its conversion into a Christian
church, the establishment of public education,
cleaner diet, a new division of labor and of land,
laws of love for laws of property;— I say to you
plainly there is no end to which your practical fac
ulty can aim, so sacred or so large, that, if pursued
for itself, will not at last become carrion and an offence to the nostril. The imaginative faculty of
the soul must be fed with objects immense and
eternal. Your end should be one inapprehensible
to the senses; then will it be a god always approached, never touched; always giving health. A
man adorns himself with prayer and love, as an

aim adorns an action. What is strong but goodness, and what is energetic but the presence of a
brave man? The doctrine in vegetable physiology
of the *presence*, or the general influence of any
substance over and above its chemical influence, as
of an alkali or a living plant, is more predicable of
man. You need not speak to me, I need not go
where you are, that you should exert magnetism on
me. Be you only whole and sufficient, and I shall
feel you in every part of my life and fortune, and
I can as easily dodge the gravitation of the globe
as escape your influence.

But there are other examples of this total and
supreme influence, besides Nature and the conscience. " From the poisonous tree, the world,"
say the Brahmins, " two species of fruit are produced, sweet as the waters of life; Love or the society of beautiful souls, and Poetry, whose taste is
like the immortal juice of Vishnu." What is Love,
and why is it the chief good, but because it is an
overpowering enthusiasm? Never self-possessed or
prudent, it is all abandonment. Is it not a certain
admirable wisdom, preferable to all other advantages, and whereof all others are only secondaries
and indemnities, because this is that in which the individual is no longer his own foolish master, but inhales an odorous and celestial air, is wrapped round
with awe of the object, blending for the time that

object with the real and only good, and consults every omen in nature with tremulous interest? When we speak truly, — is not he only unhappy who is not in love? his fancied freedom and self-rule — is it not so much death? He who is in love is wise and is becoming wiser, sees newly every time he looks at the object beloved, drawing from it with his eyes and his mind those virtues which it possesses. Therefore if the object be not itself a living and expanding soul, he presently exhausts it. But the love remains in his mind, and the wisdom it brought him; and it craves a new and higher object. And the reason why all men honor love is because it looks up and not down; aspires and not despairs.

And what is Genius but finer love, a love impersonal, a love of the flower and perfection of things, and a desire to draw a new picture or copy of the same? It looks to the cause and life: it proceeds from within outward, whilst Talent goes from without inward. Talent finds its models, methods, and ends, in society, exists for exhibition, and goes to the soul only for power to work. Genius is its own end, and draws its means and the style of its architecture from within, going abroad only for audience and spectator, as we adapt our voice and phrase to the distance and character of the ear we speak to. All your learning of all literatures would never enable you to anticipate one of its thoughts or expressions, and yet each is natural and familiar as household words. Here about us coils forever the ancient enigma, so old and so unutterable. Behold! there is the sun, and the rain, and the rocks; the old sun, the old stones. How easy were it to describe all this fitly; yet no word can pass. Nature is a mute, and man, her articulate, speaking brother, lo! he also is a mute. Yet when Genius arrives, its speech is like a river; it has no straining to describe, more than there is straining in nature to exist. When thought is best, there is most of it. Genius sheds wisdom like perfume, and advertises us that it flows out of a deeper source than the foregoing silence, that it knows so deeply and speaks so musically, because it is itself a mutation of the thing it describes. It is sun and moon and wave and fire in music, as astronomy is thought and harmony in masses of matter.

What is all history but the work of ideas, a record of the incomputible energy which his infinite aspirations infuse into man? Has anything grand and lasting been done? Who did it? Plainly not any man, but all men: it was the prevalence and inundation of an idea. What brought the pilgrims here? One man says, civil liberty; another, the desire of founding a church; and a third discovers that the motive force was plantation and trade.

But if the Puritans could rise from the dust they could not answer. It is to be seen in what they were, and not in what they designed; it was the growth and expansion of the human race, and re-sembled herein the sequent Revolution, which was not begun in Concord, or Lexington, or Virginia, but was the overflowing of the sense of natural right in every clear and active spirit of the period. Is a man boastful and knowing, and his own mas-ter?— we turn from him without hope : but let him be filled with awe and dread before the Vast and the Divine, which uses him glad to be used, and our eye is riveted to the chain of events. What a debt is ours to that old religion which, in the childhood of most of us, still dwelt like a sabbath morning in the country of New England, teaching privation, self-denial and sorrow! A man was born not for prosperity, but to suffer for the benefit of others, like the noble rock-maple which all around our villages bleeds for the service of man. Not praise, not men's acceptance of our doing, but the spirit's holy errand through us absorbed the thought. How dignified was this ! How all that is called tal-ents and success, in our noisy capitals, becomes buzz and din before this man-worthiness ! How our friendships and the complaisances we use, shame us now ! Shall we not quit our companions, as if they were thieves and pot-companions, and betake ourselves to some desert cliff of Mount Katahdin, some unvisited recess in Moosehead Lake, to bewail our innocency and to recover it, and with it the power to communicate again with these sharers of a more sacred idea?

And what is to replace for us the piety of that race? We cannot have theirs; it glides away from us day by day; but we also can bask in the great morning which rises forever out of the eastern sea, and be ourselves the children of the light. I stand here to say, Let us worship the mighty and transcendent Soul. It is the office, I doubt not, of this age to annul that adulterous divorce which the superstition of many ages has effected between the intellect and holiness. The lovers of goodness have been one class, the students of wisdom another; as if either could exist in any purity without the other. Truth is always holy, holiness always wise. I will that we keep terms with sin and a sinful literature and society no longer, but live a life of discovery and performance. Accept the intellect, and it will accept us. Be the lowly ministers of that pure omniscience, and deny it not before men. It will burn up all profane literature, all base current opinions, all the false powers of the world, as in a moment of time. I draw from nature the lesson of an intimate divinity. Our health and reason as men need our respect to this fact, against the heedlessness **and** against the contradiction of society. The sanity of man needs the poise of this immanent force. His nobility needs the assurance of this inexhaustible reserved power. How great soever have been its bounties, they are a drop to the sea whence they flow. If you say, 'The acceptance of the vision is also the act of God:'—I shall not seek to penetrate the mystery, I admit the force of what you say. If you ask, 'How can any rules be given for the attainment of gifts so sublime?' I shall only remark that the solicitations of this spirit, as long as there is life, are never forborne. Tenderly, tenderly, they woo and court us from every object in nature, from every fact in life, from every thought in the mind. The one condition coupled with the gift of truth is its use. That man shall be learned who reduceth his learning to practice. Emanuel Swedenborg affirmed that it was opened to him "that the spirits who knew truth in this life, but did it not, at death shall lose their knowledge." "If knowledge," said Ali the Caliph, "calleth unto practice, well; if not, it goeth away." The only way into nature is to enact our best insight. Instantly we are higher poets, and can speak a deeper law. Do what you know, and perception is converted into character, as islands and continents were built by invisible infusories, or as these forest leaves absorb light, electricity, and volatile gases, and the

gnarled oak to live a thousand years is the arrest
and fixation of the most volatile and ethereal currents. The doctrine of this Supreme Presence is a
cry of joy and exultation. Who shall dare think
he has come late into nature, or has missed anything excellent in the past, who seeth the admirable
stars of possibility, and the yet untouched continent
of hope glittering with all its mountains in the vast
West? I praise with wonder this great reality,
which seems to drown all things in the deluge of its
light. What man seeing this, can lose it from his
thoughts, or entertain a meaner subject? The entrance of this into his mind seems to be the birth
of man. We cannot describe the natural history
of the soul, but we know that it is divine. I cannot tell if these wonderful qualities which house to-
day in this mortal frame shall ever re-assemble in
equal activity in a similar frame, or whether they
have before had a natural history like that of this
body you see before you; but this one thing I know,
that these qualities did not now begin to exist, cannot be sick with my sickness, nor buried in any
grave; but that they circulate through the Universe:
before the world was, they were. Nothing can bar
them out, or shut them in, but they penetrate the
ocean and land, space and time, form an essence,
and hold the key to universal nature. I draw from
this faith, courage and hope. All things are known

to the soul. It is not to be surprised by any communication. Nothing can be greater than it. Let those fear and those fawn who will. The soul is in her native realm, and it is wider than space, older than time, wide as hope, rich as love. Pusillanimity and fear she refuses with a beautiful scorn; they are not for her who puts on her coronation robes, and goes out through universal love to universal power.

MAN THE REFORMER.

A LECTURE READ BEFORE THE MECHANICS' APPRENTICES'
LIBRARY ASSOCIATION, BOSTON, JANUARY 25, 1841.

MAN THE REFORMER.

Mr. President, and Gentlemen,

I wish to offer to your consideration some thoughts on the particular and general relations of man as a reformer. I shall assume that the aim of each young man in this association is the very highest that belongs to a rational mind. Let it be granted that our life, as we lead it, is common and mean; that some of those offices and functions for which we were mainly created are grown so rare in society that the memory of them is only kept alive in old books and in dim traditions; that prophets and poets, that beautiful and perfect men we are not now, no, nor have even seen such; that some sources of human instruction are almost unnamed and unknown among us; that the community in which we live will hardly bear to be told that every man should be open to ecstasy or a divine illumination, and his daily walk elevated by inter-course with the spiritual world. Grant all this, as we must, yet I suppose none of my auditors will deny that we ought to seek to establish ourselves

in such disciplines and courses as will deserve that
guidance and clearer communication with the spiritual nature.   And further, I will not dissemble
my hope that each person whom I address has felt
his own call to cast aside all evil customs, timidi-
ties, and limitations, and to be in his place a free
and helpful man, a reformer, a benefactor, not content to slip along through the world like a footman
or a spy, escaping by his nimbleness and apologies
as many knocks as he can, but a brave and upright
man, who must find or cut a straight road to
everything excellent in the earth, and not only go
honorably himself, but make it easier for all who
follow him to go in honor and with benefit.

In the history of the world the doctrine of Reform had never such scope as at the present hour.
Lutherans, Hernhutters, Jesuits, Monks, Quakers,
Knox, Wesley, Swedenborg, Bentham, in their
accusations of society, all respected something,
— church or state, literature or history, domestic
usages, the market town, the dinner table, coined
money.   But now all these and all things else hear
the trumpet, and must rush to judgment, — Christianity, the laws, commerce, schools, the farm, the
laboratory ; and not a kingdom, town, statute, rite,
calling, man, or woman, but is threatened by the
new spirit.

What if some of the objections whereby our institutions are assailed are extreme and speculative, and the reformers tend to idealism? That only shows the extravagance of the abuses which have driven the mind into the opposite extreme. It is when your facts and persons grow unreal and fantastic by too much falsehood, that the scholar flies for refuge to the world of ideas, and aims to recruit and replenish nature from that source. Let ideas establish their legitimate sway again in society, let life be fair and poetic, and the scholars will gladly be lovers, citizens, and philanthropists.

It will afford no security from the new ideas, that the old nations, the laws of centuries, the property and institutions of a hundred cities, are built on other foundations. The demon of reform has a secret door into the heart of every lawmaker, of every inhabitant of every city. The fact that a new thought and hope have dawned in your breast, should apprise you that in the same hour a new light broke in upon a thousand private hearts. That secret which you would fain keep, — as soon as you go abroad, lo! there is one standing on the doorstep to tell you the same. There is not the most bronzed and sharpened money-catcher who does not, to your consternation almost, quail and shake the moment he hears a question prompted by the new ideas. We thought he had some semblance of ground to stand upon, that such as he at least would die hard; but he trembles and flees. Then the scholar says, 'Cities and coaches shall never impose on me again; for behold every solitary dream of mine is rushing to fulfilment. That fancy I had, and hesitated to utter because you would laugh, — the broker, the attorney, the market-man are saying the same thing. Had I waited a day longer to speak, I had been too late. Behold, State Street thinks, and Wall Street doubts, and begins to prophesy!'

It cannot be wondered at that this general inquest into abuses should arise in the bosom of society, when one considers the practical impediments that stand in the way of virtuous young men. The young man, on entering life, finds the way to lucrative employments blocked with abuses. The ways of trade are grown selfish to the borders of theft, and supple to the borders (if not beyond the borders) of fraud. The employments of commerce are not intrinsically unfit for a man, or less genial to his faculties; but these are now in their general course so vitiated by derelictions and abuses at which all connive, that it requires more vigor and resources than can be expected of every young man, to right himself in them; he is lost in them; he cannot move hand or foot in them. Has he genius and virtue? the less does he find them fit for him to grow in, and if he would thrive in them, he must sacrifice all the brilliant dreams of boyhood and youth as dreams; he must forget the prayers of his childhood and must take on him the harness of routine and obsequiousness. If not so minded, nothing is left him but to begin the world anew, as he does who puts the spade into the ground for food. We are all implicated of course in this charge; it is only necessary to ask a few questions as to the progress of the articles of commerce from the fields where they grew, to our houses, to become aware that we eat and drink and wear perjury and fraud in a hundred commodities. How many articles of daily consumption are furnished us from the West Indies; yet it is said that in the Spanish islands the venality of the officers of the government has passed into usage, and that no article passes into our ships which has not been fraudulently cheapened. In the Spanish islands, every agent or factor of the Americans, unless he be a consul, has taken oath that he is a Catholic, or has caused a priest to make that declaration for him. The abolitionist has shown us our dreadful debt to the southern negro. In the island of Cuba, in addition to the ordinary abominations of slavery, it appears only men are bought for the plantations, and one dies in ten every year, of these miserable bachelors, to yield us sugar. I leave for those who have the knowledge the part of sifting the oaths of our custom-houses; I will not inquire into the oppression of the sailors; I will not pry into the usages of our retail trade. I content myself with the fact that the general system of our trade (apart from the blacker traits, which, I hope, are exceptions denounced and unshared by all reputable men), is a system of selfishness; is not dictated by the high sentiments of human nature; is not measured by the exact law of reciprocity, much less by the sentiments of love and heroism, but is a system of distrust, of concealment, of superior keenness, not of giving but of taking advantage. It is not that which a man delights to unlock to a noble friend; which he meditates on with joy and self-approval in his hour of love and aspiration; but rather what he then puts out of sight, only showing the brilliant result, and atoning for the manner of acquiring, by the manner of expending it. I do not charge the merchant or the manufacturer. The sins of our trade belong to no class, to no individual. One plucks, one distributes, one eats. Every body partakes, every body confesses, — with cap and knee volunteers his confession, yet none feels himself accountable. He did not create the abuse; he cannot alter it. What is he? an obscure private person who must get his bread. That is the vice, — that no one feels himself called to act for man, but only as a fraction of man. It happens therefore that all such ingenuous souls as feel within themselves the irrepressible strivings of a noble aim, who by the law of their nature must act simply, find these ways of trade unfit for them, and they come forth from it. Such cases are becoming more numerous every year.

But by coming out of trade you have not cleared yourself. The trail of the serpent reaches into all the lucrative professions and practices of man. Each has its own wrongs. Each finds a tender and very intelligent conscience a disqualification for success. Each requires of the practitioner a certain shutting of the eyes, a certain dapperness and compliance, an acceptance of customs, a sequestration from the sentiments of generosity and love, a compromise of private opinion and lofty integrity. Nay, the evil custom reaches into the whole institution of property, until our laws which establish and protect it seem not to be the issue of love and reason, but of selfishness. Suppose a man is so unhappy as to be born a saint, with keen perceptions but with the conscience and love of an angel, and he is to get his living in the world; he finds himself excluded from all lucrative works; he has no farm, and he cannot get one; for to earn money enough to buy one requires a sort of concentration toward money, which is the selling himself

for a number of years, and to him the present hour
is as sacred and inviolable as any future hour.
Of course, whilst another man has no land, my
title to mine, your title to yours, is at once vitiated.
Inextricable seem to be the twinings and tendrils
of this evil, and we all involve ourselves in it the
deeper by forming connections, by wives and children, by benefits and debts.

Considerations of this kind have turned the attention of many philanthropic and intelligent persons to the claims of manual labor, as a part of
the education of every young man. If the accumulated wealth of the past generation is thus tainted,
— no matter how much of it is offered to us, — we
must begin to consider if it were not the nobler
part to renounce it, and to put ourselves into primary relations with the soil and nature, and ab-
staining from whatever is dishonest and unclean,
to take each of us bravely his part, with his own
hands, in the manual labor of the world.

But it is said, ' What! will you give up the immense advantages reaped from the division of labor, and set every man to make his own shoes, bu-
reau, knife, wagon, sails, and needle ? This would
be to put men back into barbarism by their own
act.' I see no instant prospect of a virtuous revolution ; yet I confess I should not be pained at a
change which threatened a loss of some of the lux-

uries or conveniences of society, if it proceeded from a preference of the agricultural life out of the belief that our primary duties as men could be better discharged in that calling. Who could regret to see a high conscience and a purer taste exercising a sensible effect on young men in their choice of occupation, and thinning the ranks of competition in the labors of commerce, of law, and of state? It is easy to see that the inconvenience would last but a short time. This would be great action, which always opens the eyes of men. When many persons shall have done this, when the majority shall admit the necessity of reform in all these institutions, their abuses will be redressed, and the way will be open again to the advantages which arise from the division of labor, and a man may select the fittest employment for his peculiar talent again, without compromise.

But quite apart from the emphasis which the times give to the doctrine that the manual labor of society ought to be shared among all the members, there are reasons proper to every individual why he should not be deprived of it. The use of manual labor is one which never grows obsolete, and which is inapplicable to no person. A man should have a farm or a mechanical craft for his culture. We must have a basis for our higher accomplishments, our delicate entertainments of poetry and philosophy, in the work of our hands. We must have an antagonism in the tough world for all the variety of our spiritual faculties, or they will not be born. Manual labor is the study of the external world. The advantage of riches remains with him who procured them, not with the heir. When I go into my garden with a spade, and dig a bed, I feel such an exhilaration and health that I discover that I have been defrauding myself all this time in letting others do for me what I should have done with my own hands. But not only health, but education is in the work. Is it possible that I, who get indefinite quantities of sugar, hominy, cotton, buckets, crockery ware, and letter-paper, by simply signing my name once in three months to a cheque in favor of John Smith & Co. traders, get the fair share of exercise to my faculties by that act which nature intended for me in making all these far-fetched matters important to my comfort? It is Smith himself, and his carriers, and dealers, and manufacturers; it is the sailor, the hidedrogher, the butcher, the negro, the hunter, and the planter, who have intercepted the sugar of the sugar, and the cotton of the cotton. They have got the education, I only the commodity. This were all very well if I were necessarily absent, being detained by work of my own, like theirs, work of the same faculties; then should I be sure of my hands and feet; but now

I feel some shame before my wood-chopper, my ploughman, and my cook, for they have some sort of self-sufficiency, they can contrive without my aid to bring the day and year round, but I depend on them, and have not earned by use a right to my arms and feet.

Consider further the difference between the first and second owner of property. Every species of property is preyed on by its own enemies, as iron by rust; timber by rot; cloth by moths; provisions by mould, putridity, or vermin; money by thieves; an orchard by insects; a planted field by weeds and the inroad of cattle; a stock of cattle by hunger; a road by rain and frost; a bridge by freshets. And whoever takes any of these things into his possession, takes the charge of defending them from this troop of enemies, or of keeping them in repair. A man who supplies his own want, who builds a raft or a boat to go a-fishing, finds it easy to caulk it, or put in a thole-pin, or mend the rudder. What he gets only as fast as he wants for his own ends, does not embarrass him, or take away his sleep with looking after. But when he comes to give all the goods he has year after year collected, in one estate to his son, — house, orchard, ploughed land, cattle, bridges, hardware, wooden-ware, carpets, cloths, provisions, books, money, — and cannot give him the skill and experience which made or collected these, and the method and place they have in his own life, the son finds his hands full, — not to use these things, but to look after them and defend them from their natural enemies. To him they are not means, but masters. Their enemies will not remit; rust, mould, vermin, rain, sun, freshet, fire, all seize their own, fill him with vexation, and he is converted from the owner into a watchman or a watch-dog to this magazine of old and new chattels. What a change! Instead of the masterly good humor and sense of power and fertility of resource in himself; instead of those strong and learned hands, those piercing and learned eyes, that supple body, and that mighty and prevailing heart which the father had, whom nature loved and feared, whom snow and rain, water and land, beast and fish seemed all to know and to serve, — we have now a puny, protected person, guarded by walls and curtains, stoves and down beds, coaches, and men - servants and women - servants from the earth and the sky, and who, bred to depend on all these, is made anxious by all that endangers those possessions, and is forced to spend so much time in guarding them, that he has quite lost sight of their original use, namely, to help him to his ends, — to the prosecution of his love; to the helping of his friend, to the worship of his God, to the enlargement of his knowledge, to the serving of his country, to the indulgence of his sentiment ; and he is now what is called a rich man, — the menial and runner of his riches.

Hence it happens that the whole interest of history lies in the fortunes of the poor. Knowledge, Virtue, Power are the victories of man over his necessities, his march to the dominion of the world. Every man ought to have this opportunity to conquer the world for himself. Only such persons interest us, Spartans, Romans, Saracens, English, Americans, who have stood in the jaws of need, and have by their own wit and might extricated themselves, and made man victorious.

I do not wish to overstate this doctrine of labor, or insist that every man should be a farmer, any more than that every man should be a lexicographer. In general one may say that the husbandman's is the oldest and most universal profession, and that where a man does not yet discover in himself any fitness for one work more than another, this may be preferred. But the doctrine of the Farm is merely this, that every man ought to stand in primary relations with the work of the world ; ought to do it himself, and not to suffer the accident of his having a purse in his pocket, or his having been bred to some dishonorable and injurious craft, to sever him from those duties ; and for this reason, that labor is God's education ; that he only is a sincere learner, he only can become a master, who learns the secrets of labor, and who, by real cunning extorts from nature its sceptre.

Neither would I shut my ears to the plea of the learned professions, of the poet, the priest, the law-giver, and men of study generally; namely, that in the experience of all men of that class, the amount of manual labor which is necessary to the mainte-nance of a family, indisposes and disqualifies for intellectual exertion. I know, it often, perhaps usually happens that where there is a fine organ-ization, apt for poetry and philosophy, that individ-ual finds himself compelled to wait on his thoughts; to waste several days that he may enhance and glo-rify one; and is better taught by a moderate and dainty exercise, such as rambling in the fields, row-ing, skating, hunting, than by the downright drudg-ery of the farmer and the smith. I would not quite forget the venerable counsel of the Egyptian mys-teries, which declared that " there were two pairs of eyes in man, and it is requisite that the pair which are beneath should be closed, when the pair that are above them perceive, and that when the pair above are closed, those which are beneath should be opened." Yet I will suggest that no separation from labor can be without some loss of power and of truth to the seer himself; that, I doubt not, the faults and vices of our literature and philosophy, their too great fineness, effeminacy, and melancholy, are attributable to the enervated and sickly habits of the literary class. Better that the book should not be quite so good, and the book-maker abler and better, and not himself often a ludicrous contrast to all that he has written.

But granting that for ends so sacred and dear some relaxation must be had, I think that if a man find in himself any strong bias to poetry, to art, to the contemplative life, drawing him to these things with a devotion incompatible with good husbandry, that man ought to reckon early with himself, and, respecting the compensations of the Universe, ought to ransom himself from the duties of economy by a certain rigor and privation in his habits. For privileges so rare and grand, let him not stint to pay a great tax. Let him be a cænobite, a pauper, and if need be, celibate also. Let him learn to eat his meals standing, and to relish the taste of fair water and black bread. He may leave to others the costly conveniences of housekeeping, and large hospitality, and the possession of works of art. Let him feel that genius is a hospitality, and that he who can create works of art needs not collect them. He must live in a chamber, and postpone his self-indulgence, forewarned and forearmed against that frequent misfortune of men of genius, — the taste for luxury. This is the tragedy of genius; — attempt-

ing to drive along the ecliptic with one horse of the
heavens and one horse of the earth, there is only
discord and ruin and downfall to chariot and char-
ioteer.

The duty that every man should assume his own
vows, should call the institutions of society to account, and examine their fitness to him, gains in
emphasis if we look at our modes of living. Is our
housekeeping sacred and honorable? Does it raise
and inspire us, or does it cripple us instead? I
ought to be armed by every part and function of
my household, by all my social function, by my
economy, by my feasting, by my voting, by my traffic. Yet I am almost no party to any of these
things. Custom does it for me, gives me no power
therefrom, and runs me in debt to boot. We spend
our incomes for paint and paper, for a hundred
trifles, I know not what, and not for the things of
a man. Our expense is almost all for conformity.
It is for cake that we run in debt; it is not the intellect, not the heart, not beauty, not worship, that
costs so much. Why needs any man be rich?
Why must he have horses, fine garments, handsome
apartments, access to public houses and places of
amusement? Only for want of thought. Give his
mind a new image, and he flees into a solitary garden or garret to enjoy it, and is richer with that
dream than the fee of a county could make him.

But we are first thoughtless, and then find that we are moneyless. We are first sensual, and then must be rich. We dare not trust our wit for making our house pleasant to our friend, and so we buy ice-creams. He is accustomed to carpets, and we have not sufficient character to put floor cloths out of his mind whilst he stays in the house, and so we pile the floor with carpets. Let the house rather be a temple of the Furies of Lacedæmon, formidable and holy to all, which none but a Spartan may enter or so much as behold. As soon as there is faith, as soon as there is society, comfits and cushions will be left to slaves. Expense will be inventive and heroic. We shall eat hard and lie hard, we shall dwell like the ancient Romans in narrow tenements, whilst our public edifices, like theirs, will be worthy for their proportion of the landscape in which we set them, for conversation, for art, for music, for worship. We shall be rich to great purposes; poor only for selfish ones.

Now what help for these evils? How can the man who has learned but one art, procure all the conveniences of life honestly? Shall we say all we think? — Perhaps with his own hands. Suppose he collects or makes them ill; — yet he has learned their lesson. If he cannot do that? — Then perhaps he can go without. Immense wisdom and riches are in that. It is better to go with·

out, than to have them at too great a cost.   Let us
learn the meaning of economy.   Economy is a
high, humane office, a sacrament, when its aim is
grand ; when it is the prudence of simple tastes,
when it is practised for freedom, or love, or devotion.   Much of the economy which we see in houses
is of a base origin, and is best kept out of sight.
Parched corn eaten to-day, that I may have roast
fowl to my dinner on Sunday, is a baseness ; but
parched corn and a house with one apartment, that
I may be free of all perturbations, that I may be
serene and docile to what the mind shall speak,
and girt and road-ready for the lowest mission of
knowledge or goodwill, is frugality for gods and
heroes.

Can we not learn the lesson of self-help ?   Society is full of infirm people, who incessantly summon others to serve them.   They contrive everywhere to exhaust for their single comfort the entire
means and appliances of that luxury to which our
invention has yet attained.   Sofas, ottomans, stoves,
wine, game-fowl, spices, perfumes, rides, the theatre, entertainments, — all these they want, they
need, and whatever can be suggested more than
these they crave also, as if it was the bread which
should keep them from starving ; and if they miss
any one, they represent themselves as the most
wronged and most wretched persons on earth.

One must have been born and bred with them to know how to prepare a meal for their learned stomach. Meantime they never bestir themselves to serve another person; not they! they have a great deal more to do for themselves than they can possibly perform, nor do they once perceive the cruel joke of their lives, but the more odious they grow, the sharper is the tone of their complaining and craving. Can anything be so elegant as to have few wants and to serve them one's self, so as to have somewhat left to give, instead of being always prompt to grab? It is more elegant to answer one's own needs than to be richly served; inelegant perhaps it may look to-day, and to a few, but it is an elegance forever and to all.

I do not wish to be absurd and pedantic in reform. I do not wish to push my criticism on the state of things around me to that extravagant mark that shall compel me to suicide, or to an absolute isolation from the advantages of civil society. If we suddenly plant our foot and say, — I will neither eat nor drink nor wear nor touch any food or fabric which I do not know to be innocent, or deal with any person whose whole manner of life is not clear and rational, we shall stand still. Whose is so? Not mine; not thine; not his. But I think we must clear ourselves each one by the interrogation, whether we have earned our bread to-day by the hearty contribution of our energies to the common benefit; and we must not cease to *tend* to the correction of flagrant wrongs, by laying one stone aright every day.

But the idea which now begins to agitate society has a wider scope than our daily employments, our households, and the institutions of property. We are to revise the whole of our social structure, the State, the school, religion, marriage, trade, science, and explore their foundations in our own nature; we are to see that the world not only fitted the former men, but fits us, and to clear ourselves of every usage which has not its roots in our own mind. What is a man born for but to be a Reformer, a Re-maker of what man has made; a renouncer of lies; a restorer of truth and good, imitating that great Nature which embosoms us all, and which sleeps no moment on an old past, but every hour repairs herself, yielding us every morning a new day, and with every pulsation a new life? Let him renounce everything which is not true to him, and put all his practices back on their first thoughts, and do nothing for which he has not the whole world for his reason. If there are inconveniences and what is called ruin in the way, because we have so enervated and maimed ourselves, yet it would be like dying of perfumes to sink in the effort to re-attach the deeds of every day to the holy and mysterious recesses of life.

The power which is at once spring and regulator in all efforts of reform is the conviction that there is an infinite worthiness in man, which will appear at the call of worth, and that all particular reforms are the removing of some impediment. Is it not the highest duty that man should be honored in us? I ought not to allow any man, because he has broad lands, to feel that he is rich in my presence. I ought to make him feel that I can do without his riches, that I cannot be bought, — neither by comfort, neither by pride, — and though I be utterly penniless, and receiving bread from him, that he is the poor man beside me. And if, at the same time, a woman or a child discovers a sentiment of piety, or a juster way of thinking than mine, I ought to confess it by my respect and obedience, though it go to alter my whole way of life.

The Americans have many virtues, but they have not Faith and Hope. I know no two words whose meaning is more lost sight of. We use these words as if they were as obsolete as Selah and Amen. And yet they have the broadest meaning, and the most cogent application to Boston in this year. The Americans have little faith. They rely on the power of a dollar ; they are deaf to a sentiment. They think you may talk the north wind down as easily as raise society ; and no class more faithless than the scholars or intellectual men.

Now if I talk with a sincere wise man, and my
friend, with a poet, with a conscientious youth
who is still under the dominion of his own wild
thoughts, and not yet harnessed in the team of society to drag with us all in the ruts of custom, I
see at once how paltry is all this generation of un-
believers, and what a house of cards their institutions are, and I see what one brave man, what one
great thought executed might effect.   I see that
the reason of the distrust of the practical man in
all theory, is his inability to perceive the means
whereby we work.   Look, he says, at the tools with
which this world of yours is to be built.   As we
cannot make a planet, with atmosphere, rivers, and
forests, by means of the best carpenters' or engi-
neers' tools, with chemist's laboratory and smith's
forge to boot, — so neither can we ever construct
that heavenly society you prate of out of foolish,
sick, selfish men and women, such as we know
them to be.   But the believer not only beholds his
heaven to be possible, but already to begin to exist, — not by the men or materials the statesman
uses, but by men transfigured and raised above
themselves by the power of principles.   To principles something else is possible that transcends all
the power of expedients.

Every great and commanding moment in the an-
nals of the world is the triumph of some enthusiasm.

The victories of the Arabs after Mahomet, who, in a few years, from a small and mean beginning, established a larger empire than that of Rome, is an example. They did they knew not what. The naked Derar, horsed on an idea, was found an overmatch for a troop of Roman cavalry. The women fought like men, and conquered the Roman men. They were miserably equipped, miserably fed. They were Temperance troops. There was neither brandy nor flesh needed to feed them. They conquered Asia, and Africa, and Spain, on barley. The Caliph Omar's walking-stick struck more terror into those who saw it than another man's sword. His diet was barley bread; his sauce was salt; and oftentimes by way of abstinence he ate his bread without salt. His drink was water. His palace was built of mud; and when he left Medina to go to the conquest of Jerusalem, he rode on a red camel, with a wooden platter hanging at his saddle, with a bottle of water and two sacks, one holding barley, and the other dried fruits.

But there will dawn ere long on our politics, on our modes of living, a nobler morning than that Arabian faith, in the sentiment of love. This is the one remedy for all ills, the panacea of nature. We must be lovers, and at once the impossible becomes possible. Our age and history, for these thousand years, has not been the history of kindness, but

of selfishness. Our distrust is very expensive. The
money we spend for courts and prisons is very ill
laid out. We make, by distrust, the thief, and
burglar, and incendiary, and by our court and jail
we keep him so. An acceptance of the sentiment
of love throughout Christendom for a season would
bring the felon and the outcast to our side in tears,
with the devotion of his faculties to our service.
See this wide society of laboring men and women.
We allow ourselves to be served by them, we live
apart from them, and meet them without a salute
in the streets. We do not greet their talents, nor
rejoice in their good fortune, nor foster their hopes,
nor in the assembly of the people vote for what is
dear to them. Thus we enact the part of the selfish noble and king from the foundation of the
world. See, this tree always bears one fruit. In
every household, the peace of a pair is poisoned by
the malice, slyness, indolence, and alienation of do-
mestics. Let any two matrons meet, and observe
how soon their conversation turns on the troubles
from their " *help*," as our phrase is. In every
knot of laborers the rich man does not feel himself
among his friends, — and at the polls he finds them
arrayed in a mass in distinct opposition to him.
We complain that the politics of masses of the
people are controlled by designing men, and led in
opposition to manifest justice and the common

weal, and to their own interest. But the people do not wish to be represented or ruled by the ignorant and base. They only vote for these, because they were asked with the voice and semblance of kindness. They will not vote for them long. They inevitably prefer wit and probity. To use an Egyptian metaphor, it is not their will for any long time " to raise the nails of wild beasts, and to depress the heads of the sacred birds." Let our affection flow out to our fellows; it would operate in a day the greatest of all revolutions. It is better to work on institutions by the sun than by the wind. The State must consider the poor man, and all voices must speak for him. Every child that is born must have a just chance for his bread. Let the amelioration in our laws of property proceed from the concession of the rich, not from the grasping of the poor. Let us begin by habitual imparting. Let us understand that the equitable rule is, that no one should take more than his share, let him be ever so rich. Let me feel that I am to be a lover. I am to see to it that the world is the better for me, and to find my reward in the act. Love would put a new face on this weary old world in which we dwell as pagans and enemies too long, and it would warm the heart to see how fast the vain diplomacy of statesmen, the impotence of armies, and navies, and lines of defence, would be

superseded by this unarmed child. Love will creep
where it cannot go, will accomplish that by imper-
ceptible methods, — being its own lever, fulcrum,
and power, — which force could never achieve.
Have you not seen in the woods, in a late autumn
morning, a poor fungus or mushroom, — a plant
without any solidity, nay, that seemed nothing but
a soft mush or jelly, — by its constant, total, and
inconceivably gentle pushing, manage to break its
way up through the frosty ground, and actually to
lift a hard crust on its head?   It is the symbol of
the power of kindness. The virtue of this principle
in human society in application to great interests is
obsolete and forgotten.   Once or twice in history
it has been tried in illustrious instances, with signal success.   This great, overgrown, dead Christendom of ours still keeps alive at least the name
of a lover of mankind. But one day all men will be
lovers; and every calamity will be dissolved in the
universal sunshine.

Will you suffer me to add one trait more to this
portrait of man the reformer? The mediator between the spiritual and the actual world should
have a great prospective prudence. An Arabian
poet describes his hero by saying,

> "Sunshine was he
> In the winter day;
> And in the midsummer
> Coolness and shade."

He who would help himself and others should not be a subject of irregular and interrupted impulses of virtue, but a continent, persisting, immovable person, — such as we have seen a few scattered up and down in time for the blessing of the world ; men who have in the gravity of their nature a quality which answers to the fly-wheel in a mill, which distributes the motion equably over all the wheels and hinders it from falling unequally and suddenly in destructive shocks. It is better that joy should be spread over all the day in the form of strength, than that it should be concentrated into ecstasies, full of danger and followed by reactions. There is a sublime prudence which is the very highest that we know of man, which, believing in a vast future, — sure of more to come than is yet seen, — postpones always the present hour to the whole life ; postpones talent to genius, and special results to character. As the merchant gladly takes money from his income to add to his capital, so is the great man very willing to lose particular powers and talents, so that he gain in the elevation of his life. The opening of the spiritual senses disposes men ever to greater sacrifices, to leave their signal talents, their best means and skill of procuring a present success, their power and their fame, — to cast all things behind, in the insatiable thirst for divine communications. A purer fame, a greater power rewards the sacrifice. It is the conversion of our harvest into seed. As the farmer casts into the ground the finest ears of his grain, the time will come when we too shall hold nothing back, but shall eagerly convert more than we now possess into means and powers, when we shall be willing to sow the sun and the moon for seeds.

LECTURE ON THE TIMES.

READ AT THE MASONIC TEMPLE, BOSTON, DECEMBER 2, 1841.

LECTURE ON THE TIMES.

THE TIMES, as we say — or the present aspects of our social state, the Laws, Divinity, Natural Science, Agriculture, Art, Trade, Letters, have their root in an invisible spiritual reality. To appear in these aspects, they must first exist, or have some necessary foundation. Beside all the small reasons we assign, there is a great reason for the existence of every extant fact; a reason which lies grand and immovable, often unsuspected, behind it in silence. The Times are the masquerade of the Eternities; trivial to the dull, tokens of noble and majestic agents to the wise; the receptacle in which the Past leaves its history; the quarry out of which the genius of to-day is building up the Future. The Times — the nations, manners, institutions, opinions, votes, are to be studied as omens, as sacred leaves, whereon a weighty sense is inscribed, if we have the wit and the love to search it out. Nature itself seems to propound to us this topic, and to invite us to explore the meaning of the conspicuous facts of the day. Everything that is popular, it has been said, deserves the attention of the philosopher : and this for the obvious reason, that although it may not be of any worth in itself, yet it characterizes the people.

Here is very good matter to be handled, if we are skilful; an abundance of important practical questions which it behooves us to understand. Let us examine the pretensions of the attacking and defending parties. Here is this great fact of Conservatism, entrenched in its immense redoubts, with Himmaleh for its front, and Atlas for its flank, and Andes for its rear, and the Atlantic and Pacific seas for its ditches and trenches ; which has planted its crosses, and crescents, and stars and stripes, and various signs and badges of possession, over every rood of the planet, and says, 'I will hold fast; and to whom I will, will I give; and whom I will, will I exclude and starve:' so says Conservatism; and all the children of men attack the colossus in their youth, and all, or all but a few, bow before it when they are old. A necessity not yet commanded, a negative imposed on the will of man by his condition, a deficiency in his force, is the foundation on which it rests. Let this side be fairly stated. Meantime, on the other part, arises Reform, and offers the sentiment of Love as an overmatch to this material might. I wish to consider well this affirmative side, which has a loftier port and reason than heretofore, which encroaches on the other every day, puts it out of countenance, out of reason, and out of temper, and leaves it nothing but silence and possession.

The fact of aristocracy, with its two weapons of wealth and manners, is as commanding a feature of the nineteenth century and the American republic as of old Rome, or modern England. The reason and influence of wealth, the aspect of philosophy and religion, and the tendencies which have acquired the name of Transcendentalism in Old and New England; the aspect of poetry, as the exponent and interpretation of these things; the fuller development and the freer play of Character as a social and political agent; — these and other related topics will in turn come to be considered.

But the subject of the Times is not an abstract question. We talk of the world, but we mean a few men and women. If you speak of the age, you mean your own platoon of people, as Dante and Milton painted in colossal their platoons, and called them Heaven and Hell. In our idea of progress, we do not go out of this personal picture. We do not think the sky will be bluer, or honey sweeter, or our climate more temperate, but only that our relation to our fellows will be simpler and happier. What is the reason to be given for this extreme attraction which *persons* have for us, but that they

are the Age? they are the results of the Past;
they are the heralds of the Future. They indicate,
— these witty, suffering, blushing, intimidating figures of the only race in which there are individuals
or changes, how far on the Fate has gone, and what
it drives at. As trees make scenery, and constitute the hospitality of the landscape, so persons are
the world to persons. A cunning mystery by which
the Great Desert of thoughts and of planets takes
this engaging form, to bring, as it would seem, its
meanings nearer to the mind. Thoughts walk and
speak, and look with eyes at me, and transport me
into new and magnificent scenes. These are the
pungent instructors who thrill the heart of each of
us, and make all other teaching formal and cold.
How I follow them with aching heart, with pining
desire! I count myself nothing before them. I
would die for them with joy. They can do what
they will with me. How they lash us with those
tongues! How they make the tears start, make us
blush and turn pale, and lap us in Elysium to sooth-
ing dreams and castles in the air! By tones of
triumph, of dear love, by threats, by pride that
freezes, these have the skill to make the world look
bleak and inhospitable, or seem the nest of tenderness and joy. I do not wonder at the miracles
which poetry attributes to the music of Orpheus,
when I remember what I have experienced from

the varied notes of the human voice. They are an
incalculable energy which countervails all other
forces in nature, because they are the channel of
supernatural powers. There is no interest or institution so poor and withered, but if a new strong
man could be born into it, he would immediately
redeem and replace it. A personal ascendency, —
that is the only fact much worth considering. I remember, some years ago, somebody shocked a circle
of friends of order here in Boston, who supposed
that our people were identified with their religious
denominations, by declaring that an eloquent man,
— let him be of what sect soever, — would be or-
dained at once in one of our metropolitan churches.
To be sure he would; and not only in ours but in
any church, mosque, or temple, on the planet; but
he must be eloquent, able to supplant our method
and classification by the superior beauty of his own.
Every fact we have was brought here by some person; and there is none that will not change and
pass away before a person whose nature is broader
than the person which the fact in question represents. And so I find the Age walking about in
happy and hopeful natures, in strong eyes and pleasant thoughts, and think I read it nearer and truer
so, than in the statute-book, or in the investments
of capital, which rather celebrate with mournful
music the obsequies of the last age. In the brain of a

fanatic; in the wild hope of a mountain boy, called by city boys very ignorant, because they do not know what his hope has certainly apprised him shall be; in the love-glance of a girl; in the hair-splitting conscientiousness of some eccentric person who has found some new scruple to embarrass himself and his neighbors withal is to be found that which shall constitute the times to come, more than in the now organized and accredited oracles. For whatever is affirmative and now advancing, contains it. I think that only is real which men love and rejoice in; not what they tolerate, but what they choose; what they embrace and avow, and not the things which chill, benumb, and terrify them.

And so why not draw for these times a portrait gallery? Let us paint the painters. Whilst the Daguerreotypist, with camera-obscura and silver plate, begins now to traverse the land, let us set up our Camera also, and let the sun paint the people. Let us paint the agitator, and the man of the old school, and the member of Congress, and the college-professor, the formidable editor, the priest and reformer, the contemplative girl, and the fair aspirant for fashion and opportunities, the woman of the world who has tried and knows; — let us examine how well she knows. Could we indicate the indicators, indicate those who most accurately represent every good and evil tendency of the general mind, in the just order which they take on this canvas of Time, so that all witnesses should recognize a spiritual law as each well known form flitted for a moment across the wall, we should have a series of sketches which would report to the next ages the color and quality of ours.

Certainly I think if this were done there would be much to admire as well as to condemn; souls of as lofty a port as any in Greek or Roman fame might appear; men of great heart, of strong hand, and of persuasive speech; subtle thinkers, and men of wide sympathy, and an apprehension which looks over all history and everywhere recognizes its own. To be sure, there will be fragments and hints of men, more than enough: bloated promises, which end in nothing or little. And then truly great men, but with some defect in their composition which neutralizes their whole force. Here is a Damascus blade, such as you may search through nature in vain to parallel, laid up on the shelf in some village to rust and ruin. And how many seem not quite available for that idea which they represent? Now and then comes a bolder spirit, I should rather say, a more surrendered soul, more informed and led by God, which is much in advance of the rest, quite beyond their sympathy, but predicts what shall soon be the general fulness; as when we stand by the seashore, whilst the tide is coming in, a wave comes up the beach far higher than any foregoing one, and recedes; and for a long while none comes up to that mark; but after some time the whole sea is there and beyond it.

But we are not permitted to stand as spectators of the pageant which the times exhibit; we are parties also, and have a responsibility which is not to be declined. A little while this interval of wonder and comparison is permitted us, but to the end that we shall play a manly part. As the solar system moves forward in the heavens, certain stars open before us, and certain stars close up behind us; so is man's life. The reputations that were great and inaccessible change and tarnish. How great were once Lord Bacon's dimensions! he is now reduced almost to the middle height; and many another star has turned out to be a planet or an asteroid: only a few are the fixed stars which have no parallax, or none for us. The change and decline of old reputations are the gracious marks of our own growth. Slowly, like light of morning, it steals on us, the new fact, that we who were pupils or aspirants are now society: do compose a portion of that head and heart we are wont to think worthy of all reverence and heed. We are the representatives of religion and intellect, and stand in the light of Ideas, whose rays stream through us to those younger and more in the dark. What further relations we sustain, what new lodges we are entering, is now unknown. To-day is a king in disguise. To-day always looks mean to the thoughtless, in the face of an uniform experience that all good and great and happy actions are made up precisely of these blank to-days. Let us not be so deceived. Let us unmask the king as he passes. Let us not inhabit times of wonderful and various promise without divining their tendency. Let us not see the foundations of nations, and of a new and better order of things laid, with roving eyes, and an attention preoccupied with trifles.

The two omnipresent parties of History, the party of the Past and the party of the Future, divide society to-day as of old. Here is the innumerable multitude of those who accept the state and the church from the last generation, and stand on no argument but possession. They have reason also, and, as I think, better reason than is commonly stated. No Burke, no Metternich has yet done full justice to the side of conservatism. But this class, however large, relying not on the intellect but on the instinct, blends itself with the brute forces of nature, is respectable only as nature is; but the individuals have no attraction for us. It is the dissenter, the theorist, the aspirant, who is quitting this ancient domain to embark on seas of adventure, who engages our interest. Omitting then for the present all notice of the stationary class, we shall find that the movement party divides itself into two classes, the actors, and the students.

The actors constitute that great army of martyrs who, at least in America, by their conscience and philanthropy, occupy the ground which Calvinism occupied in the last age, and compose the visible church of the existing generation. The present age will be marked by its harvest of projects for the reform of domestic, civil, literary, and ecclesiastical institutions. The leaders of the crusades against War, Negro slavery, Intemperance, Government based on force, Usages of trade, Court and Custom-house Oaths, and so on to the agitators on the system of Education and the laws of Property, are the right successors of Luther, Knox, Robinson, Fox, Penn, Wesley, and Whitfield. They have the same virtues and vices; the same noble impulse, and the same bigotry. These movements are on all accounts important; they not only check the special abuses, but they educate the conscience and the intellect of the people. How can such a question as the Slave-trade be agitated for forty years by all the Christian nations, without throwing great light on ethics into the general mind? The fury with which the slave-trader defends every inch of his bloody deck and his howling auction-platform, is a trumpet to alarm the ear of mankind, to wake the dull, and drive all neutrals to take sides and to listen to the argument and the verdict. The Temperance-question, which rides the conversation of ten thousand circles, and is tacitly recalled at every public and at every private table, drawing with it all the curious ethics of the Pledge, of the Wine-question, of the equity of the manufacture and the trade, is a gymnastic training to the casuistry and conscience of the time. Anti-masonry had a deep right and wrong, which gradually emerged to sight out of the turbid controversy. The political questions touching the Banks; the Tariff; the limits of the executive power; the right of the constituent to instruct the representative; the treatment of the Indians; the Boundary wars; the Congress of nations; are all pregnant with ethical conclusions; and it is well if government and our social order can extricate themselves from these alembics and find themselves still government and social order. The student of history will hereafter compute the singular value of our endless discussion of questions to the mind of the period.

Whilst each of these aspirations and attempts of the people for the Better is magnified by the natural exaggeration of its advocates, until it excludes the others from sight, and repels discreet persons by the unfairness of the plea, the movements are in reality all parts of one movement. There is a

perfect chain, — see it, or see it not, — of reforms
emerging from the surrounding darkness, each
cherishing some part of the general idea, and all
must be seen in order to do justice to any one.
Seen in this their natural connection, they are sublime. The conscience of the Age demonstrates itself in this effort to raise the life of man by putting
it in harmony with his idea of the Beautiful and
the Just. The history of reform is always identical, it is the comparison of the idea with the fact.
Our modes of living are not agreeable to our imagination. We suspect they are unworthy. We arraign our daily employments. They appear to us
unfit, unworthy of the faculties we spend on them.
In conversation with a wise man, we find ourselves
apologizing for our employments ; we speak of
them with shame. Nature, literature, science,
childhood, appear to us beautiful; but not our own
daily work, not the ripe fruit and considered labors
of man. This beauty which the fancy finds in
everything else, certainly accuses the manner of
life we lead. Why should it be hateful ? Why
should it contrast thus with all natural beauty ?
Why should it not be poetic, and invite and raise
us ? Is there a necessity that the works of man
should be sordid ? Perhaps not. — Out of this fair
Idea in the mind springs the effort at the Perfect.
It is the interior testimony to a fairer possibility of

life and manners which agitates society every day with the offer of some new amendment. If we would make more strict inquiry concerning its origin, we find ourselves rapidly approaching the inner boundaries of thought, that term where speech becomes silence, and science conscience. For the origin of all reform is in that mysterious fountain of the moral sentiment in man, which, amidst the natural, ever contains the supernatural for men. That is new and creative. That is alive. That alone can make a man other than he is. Here or nowhere resides unbounded energy, unbounded power.

The new voices in the wilderness crying " Repent," have revived a hope, which had well-nigh perished out of the world, that the thoughts of the mind may yet, in some distant age, in some happy hour, be executed by the hands. That is the hope, of which all other hopes are parts. For some ages, these ideas have been consigned to the poet and musical composer, to the prayers and the sermons of churches; but the thought that they can ever have any footing in real life, seems long since to have been exploded by all judicious persons. Milton, in his best tract, describes a relation between religion and the daily occupations, which is true until this time.

" A wealthy man, addicted to his pleasure and

to his profits, finds religion to be a traffic so entangled, and of so many piddling accounts, that of all mysteries he cannot skill to keep a stock going upon that trade. What should he do? Fain he would have the name to be religious; fain he would bear up with his neighbors in that. What does he therefore, but resolve to give over toiling, and to find himself out some factor, to whose care and credit he may commit the whole managing of his religious affairs; some divine of note and estimation that must be. To him he adheres, resigns the whole warehouse of his religion, with all the locks and keys, into his custody; and indeed makes the very person of that man his religion; esteems his associating with him a sufficient evidence and commendatory of his own piety. So that a man may say his religion is now no more within himself, but is become a dividual moveable, and goes and comes near him, according as that good man frequents the house. He entertains him, gives him gifts, feasts him, lodges him; his religion comes home at night, prays, is liberally supped, and sumptuously laid to sleep; rises, is saluted, and after the malmsey, or some well spiced bruage, and better breakfasted than he whose morning appetite would have gladly fed on green figs between Bethany and Jerusalem, his religion walks abroad at eight, and leaves his kind entertainer in the shop, trading all day without his religion."

This picture would serve for our times. Religion was not invited to eat or drink or sleep with us,
or to make or divide an estate, but was a holiday
guest. Such omissions judge the church ; as the
compromise made with the slaveholder, not much
noticed at first, every day appears more flagrant
mischief to the American constitution. But now
the purists are looking into all these matters. The
more intelligent are growing uneasy on the subject
of Marriage. They wish to see the character represented also in that covenant. There shall be
nothing brutal in it, but it shall honor the man and
the woman, as much as the most diffusive and universal action. Grimly the same spirit looks into
the law of Property, and accuses men of driving a
trade in the great boundless providence which had
given the air, the water, and the land to men, to
use and not to fence in and monopolize. It casts
its eye on Trade, and Day Labor, and so it goes up
and down, paving the earth with eyes, destroying
privacy and making thorough-lights. Is all this for
nothing ? Do you suppose that the reforms which
are preparing will be as superficial as those we
know ?

By the books it reads and translates, judge what
books it will presently print. A great deal of the
profoundest thinking of antiquity, which had become as good as obsolete for us, is now re-appear-

ing in extracts and allusions, and in twenty years will get all printed anew. See how daring is the reading, the speculation, the experimenting of the time. If now some genius shall arise who could unite these scattered rays! And always such a genius does embody the ideas of each time. Here is great variety and richness of mysticism, each part of which now only disgusts whilst it forms the sole thought of some poor Perfectionist or " Comer out," yet when it shall be taken up as the garniture of some profound and all-reconciling thinker, will appear the rich and appropriate decoration of his robes.

These reforms are our contemporaries; they are ourselves; our own light, and sight, and conscience; they only name the relation which subsists between us and the vicious institutions which they go to rectify. They are the simplest statements of man in these matters; the plain right and wrong. I cannot choose but allow and honor them. The impulse is good, and the theory; the practice is less beautiful. The Reformers affirm the inward life, but they do not trust it, but use outward and vulgar means. They do not rely on precisely that strength which wins me to their cause; not on love, not on a principle, but on men, on multitudes, on circumstances, on money, on party; that is, on fear, on wrath, and pride. The love which lifted men to

the sight of these better ends was the true and best
distinction of this time, the disposition to trust a
principle more than a material force. I think *that*
the soul of reform ; the conviction that not sensual-
ism, not slavery, not war, not imprisonment, not
even government, are needed, — but in lieu of them
all, reliance on the sentiment of man, which will
work best the more it is trusted ; not reliance on
numbers, but, contrariwise, distrust of numbers and
the feeling that then are we strongest when most
private and alone. The young men who have been
vexing society for these last years with regenerative
methods seem to have made this mistake ; they all
exaggerated some special means, and all failed to
see that the Reform of Reforms must be accomplished without means.

The Reforms have their high origin in an ideal
justice, but they do not retain the purity of an idea.
They are quickly organized in some low, inadequate
form, and present no more poetic image to the
mind than the evil tradition which they reprobated.
They mix the fire of the moral sentiment with personal and party heats, with measureless exaggera-
tions, and the blindness that prefers some darling
measure to justice and truth. Those who are urg-
ing with most ardor what are called the greatest
benefits of mankind, are narrow, self-pleasing, con-
ceited men, and affect us as the insane do. **They**

bite us, and we run mad also. I think the work of
the reformer as innocent as other work that is done
around him; but when I have seen it near, I do
not like it better. It is done in the same way, it
is done profanely, not piously; by management, by
tactics and clamor. It is a buzz in the ear. I
cannot feel any pleasure in sacrifices which display
to me such partiality of character. We do not
want actions, but men; not a chemical drop of water, but rain; the spirit that sheds and showers actions, countless, endless actions. You have on some
occasion played a bold part. You have set your
heart and face against society when you thought it
wrong, and returned it frown for frown. Excellent: now can you afford to forget it, reckoning all
your action no more than the passing of your hand
through the air, or a little breath of your mouth?
The world leaves no track in space, and the greatest action of man no mark in the vast idea. To
the youth diffident of his ability and full of com-
punction at his unprofitable existence, the temptation is always great to lend himself to public movements, and as one of a party accomplish what he
cannot hope to effect alone. But he must resist
the degradation of a man to a measure. I must
get with truth, though I should never come to act,
as you call it, with effect. I must consent to inaction. A patience which is grand; a brave and cold

neglect of the offices which prudence exacts, so it be done in a deep upper piety; a consent to solitude and inaction which proceeds out of an unwillingness to violate character, is the century which makes the gem. Whilst therefore I desire to express the respect and joy I feel before this sublime connection of reforms now in their infancy around us, I urge the more earnestly the paramount duties of self-reliance. I cannot find language of sufficient energy to convey my sense of the sacredness of private integrity. All men, all things, the state, the church, yea the friends of the heart are phantasms and unreal beside the sanctuary of the heart. With so much awe, with so much fear, let it be respected.

The great majority of men, unable to judge of any principle until its light falls on a fact, are not aware of the evil that is around them until they see it in some gross form, as in a class of intemperate men, or slaveholders, or soldiers, or fraudulent persons. Then they are greatly moved; and magnifying the importance of that wrong, they fancy that if that abuse were redressed all would go well, and they fill the land with clamor to correct it. Hence the missionary, and other religious efforts. If every island and every house had a Bible, if every child was brought into the Sunday School, would the wounds of the world heal, and man be upright?

But the man of ideas, accounting the circumstance nothing, judges of the commonwealth from the state of his own mind. 'If,' he says, ' I am selfish, then is there slavery, or the effort to establish it, wherever I go. But if I am just, then is there no slavery, let the laws say what they will. For if I treat all men as gods, how to me can there be any such thing as a slave?' But how frivolous is your war against circumstances. This denouncing philanthropist is himself a slaveholder in every word and look. Does he free me? Does he cheer me? He is the state of Georgia, or Alabama, with their sanguinary slave-laws, walking here on our northeastern shores. We are all thankful he has no more political power, as we are fond of liberty ourselves. I am afraid our virtue is a little geographical. I am not mortified by our vice; that is obduracy; it colors and palters, it curses and swears, and I can see to the end of it; but I own our virtue makes me ashamed; so sour and narrow, so thin and blind, virtue so vice-like. Then again, how trivial seem the contests of the abolitionist, whilst he aims merely at the circumstance of the slave. Give the slave the least elevation of religious sentiment, and he is no slave ; you are the slave ; he not only in his humility feels his superiority, feels that much deplored condition of his to be a fading trifle, but he makes you feel it too. He is the master. The exaggeration which our young people make of his wrongs, characterizes themselves. What are no trifles to them, they naturally think are no trifles to Pompey.

We say then that the reforming movement is sacred in its origin ; in its management and details, timid and profane. These benefactors hope to raise man by improving his circumstances : by combination of that which is dead they hope to make something alive. In vain. By new infusions alone of the spirit by which he is made and directed, can he be re-made and reinforced. The sad Pestalozzi, who shared with all ardent spirits the hope of Europe on the outbreak of the French Revolution, after witnessing its sequel, recorded his conviction that "the amelioration of outward circumstances will be the effect but can never be the means of mental and moral improvement." Quitting now the class of actors, let us turn to see how it stands with the other class of which we spoke, namely, the students.

A new disease has fallen on the life of man. Every Age, like every human body, has its own distemper. Other times have had war, or famine, or a barbarism, domestic or bordering, as their antagonism. Our forefathers walked in the world and went to their graves tormented with the fear of Sin and the terror of the Day of Judgment.

These terrors have lost their force, and our tor-
ment is Unbelief, the Uncertainty as to what we
ought to do; the distrust of the value of what we
do, and the distrust that the Necessity (which we
all at last believe in) is fair and beneficent. Our
Religion assumes the negative form of rejection.
Out of love of the true, we repudiate the false;
and the Religion is an abolishing criticism. A
great perplexity hangs like a cloud on the brow of
all cultivated persons, a certain imbecility in the
best spirits, which distinguishes the period. We
do not find the same trait in the Arabian, in the
Hebrew, in Greek, Roman, Norman, English periods; no, but in other men a natural firmness.
The men did not see beyond the need of the
hour. They planted their foot strong, and doubted
nothing. We mistrust every step we take. We
find it the worst thing about time that we know
not what to do with it. We are so sharp-sighted
that we can neither work nor think, neither read
Plato nor not read him.

Then there is what is called a too intellectual
tendency. Can there be too much intellect? We
have never met with any such excess. But the
criticism which is levelled at the laws and manners, ends in thought, without causing a new
method of life. The genius of the day does not
incline to a deed, but to a beholding. It is not

that men do not wish to act; they pine to be employed, but are paralyzed by the uncertainty what they should do. The inadequacy of the work to the faculties is the painful perception which keeps them still. This happens to the best. Then, talents bring their usual temptations, and the current literature and poetry with perverse ingenuity draw us away from life to solitude and meditation. This could well be borne, if it were great and involuntary; if the men were ravished by their thought, and hurried into ascetic extravagances. Society could then manage to release their shoulder from its wheel and grant them for a time this privilege of sabbath. But they are not so. Thinking, which was a rage, is become an art. The thinker gives me results, and never invites me to be present with him at his invocation of truth, and to enjoy with him its proceeding into his mind.

So little action amidst such audacious and yet sincere profession, that we begin to doubt if that great revolution in the art of war, which has made it a game of posts instead of a game of battles, has not operated on Reform; whether this be not also a war of posts, a paper blockade, in which each party is to display the utmost resources of his spirit and belief, and no conflict occur, but the world shall take that course which the demonstration of the truth shall indicate.

But we must pay for being too intellectual, as they call it. People are not as light-hearted for it. I think men never loved life less. I question if care and doubt ever wrote their names so legibly on the faces of any population. This *Ennui*, for which we Saxons had no name, this word of France has got a terrific significance. It shortens life, and bereaves the day of its light. Old age begins in the nursery, and before the young American is put into jacket and trowsers, he says, 'I want something which I never saw before;' and 'I wish I was not I.' I have seen the same gloom on the brow even of those adventurers from the intellectual class who had dived deepest and with most success into active life. I have seen the authentic sign of anxiety and perplexity on the greatest forehead of the State. The canker worms have crawled to the topmost bough of the wild elm, and swing down from that. Is there less oxygen in the atmosphere? What has checked in this age the animal spirits which gave to our forefathers their bounding pulse?

But have a little patience with this melancholy humor. Their unbelief arises out of a greater Belief; their inaction out of a scorn of inadequate action. By the side of these men, the hot agitators have a certain cheap and ridiculous air; they even look smaller than the others. Of the two, I

own I like the speculators best. They have some
piety which looks with faith to a fair Future, un-
profaned by rash and unequal attempts to realize
it. And truly we shall find much to console us,
when we consider the cause of their uneasiness. It
is the love of greatness, it is the need of harmony,
the contrast of the dwarfish Actual with the exor-
bitant Idea. No man can compare the ideas and
aspirations of the innovators of the present day
with those of former periods, without feeling how
great and high this criticism is. The revolutions
that impend over society are not now from ambition and rapacity, from impatience of one or another form of government, but from new modes of
thinking, which shall recompose society after a
new order, which shall animate labor by love and
science, which shall destroy the value of many kinds
of property and replace all property within the
dominion of reason and equity. There was never
so great a thought laboring in the breasts of men
as now. It almost seems as if what was aforetime
spoken fabulously and hieroglyphically, was now
spoken plainly, the doctrine, namely, of the indwelling of the Creator in man. The spiritualist wishes
this only, that the spiritual principle should be suffered to demonstrate itself to the end, in all possible applications to the state of man, without the
admission of anything unspiritual, that is, anything

positive, dogmatic, or personal.   The excellence of
this class consists in this, that they have believed;
that, affirming the need of new and higher modes
of living and action, they have abstained from the
recommendation of low methods.   Their fault is
that they have stopped at the intellectual perception; that their will is not yet inspired from the
Fountain of Love.   But whose fault is this? and
what a fault, and to what inquiry does it lead!
We have come to that which is the spring of all
power, of beauty and virtue, of art and poetry;
and who shall tell us according to what law its inspirations and its informations are given or with-
holden?

I do not wish to be guilty of the narrowness and
pedantry of inferring the tendency and genius of
the Age from a few and insufficient facts or persons.   Every age has a thousand sides and signs
and tendencies, and it is only when surveyed from
inferior points of view that great varieties of character appear.   Our time too is full of activity and
performance.   Is there not something comprehen-
sive in the grasp of a society which to great mechanical invention and the best institutions of property
adds the most daring theories; which explores the
subtlest and most universal problems?   At the
manifest risk of repeating what every other Age
has thought of itself, we might say we think the

Genius of this Age more philosophical than any other has been, righter in its aims, truer, with less fear, less fable, less mixture of any sort.

But turn it how we will, as we ponder this meaning of the times, every new thought drives us to the deep fact that the Time is the child of the Eternity. The main interest which any aspects of the Times can have for us, is the great spirit which gazes through them, the light which they can shed on the wonderful questions, What we are? and Whither we tend? We do not wish to be deceived. Here we drift, like white sail across the wild ocean, now bright on the wave, now darkling in the trough of the sea; — but from what port did we sail? Who knows? Or to what port are we bound? Who knows? There is no one to tell us but such poor weather-tossed mariners as ourselves, whom we speak as we pass, or who have hoisted some signal, or floated to us some letter in a bottle from far. But what know they more than we? They also found themselves on this wondrous sea. No; from the older sailors, nothing. Over all their speaking-trumpets, the gray sea and the loud winds answer, Not in us; not in Time. Where then but in Ourselves, where but in that Thought through which we communicate with absolute nature, and are made aware that whilst we shed the dust of which we are built, grain by grain, till it is all gone, the law which clothes us with humanity remains anew? where but in the intuitions which are vouchsafed us from within, shall we learn the Truth? Faithless, faithless, we fancy that with the dust we depart and are not, and do not know that the law and the perception of the law are at last one; that only as much as the law enters us, becomes us, we are living men, — immortal with the immortality of this law. Underneath all these appearances lies that which is, that which lives, that which causes. This ever renewing generation of appearances rests on a reality, and a reality that is alive.

To a true scholar the attraction of the aspects of nature, the departments of life, and the passages of his experience, is simply the information they yield him of this supreme nature which lurks within all. That reality, that causing force is moral. The Moral Sentiment is but its other name. It makes by its presence or absence right and wrong, beauty and ugliness, genius or depravation. As the granite comes to the surface and towers into the highest mountains, and, if we dig down, we find it below the superficial strata, so in all the details of our domestic or civil life is hidden the elemental reality, which ever and anon comes to the surface, and forms the grand men, who are the leaders and examples, rather than the companions of the race. The granite is curiously concealed under a thousand formations and surfaces, under fertile soils, and grasses, and flowers, under well-manured, arable fields, and large towns and cities, but it makes the foundation of these, and is always indicating its presence by slight but sure signs. So is it with the Life of our life; so close does that also hide. I read it in glad and in weeping eyes; I read it in the pride and in the humility of people; it is recognized in every bargain and in every complaisance, in every criticism, and in all praise; it is voted for at elections; it wins the cause with juries; it rides the stormy eloquence of the senate, sole victor; histories are written of it, holidays decreed to it; statues, tombs, churches, built to its honor; yet men seem to fear and to shun it when it comes barely to view in our immediate neighborhood.

For that reality let us stand; that let us serve, and for that speak. Only as far as *that* shines through them are these times or any times worth consideration. I wish to speak of the politics, education, business, and religion around us without ceremony or false deference. You will absolve me from the charge of flippancy, or malignity, or the desire to say smart things at the expense of whomsoever, when you see that reality is all we prize, and that we are bound on our entrance into nature to speak for that. Let it not be recorded in our own memories that in this moment of the Eternity, when we who were named by our names flitted across the light, we were afraid of any fact, or disgraced the fair Day by a pusillanimous preference of our bread to our freedom. What is the scholar, what is the man *for*, but for hospitality to every new thought of his time? Have you leisure, power, property, friends? You shall be the asylum and patron of every new thought, every unproven opinion, every untried project which proceeds out of good will and honest seeking. All the newspapers, all the tongues of to-day will of course at first defame what is noble; but you who hold not of to-day, not of the times, but of the Everlasting, are to stand for it: and the highest compliment man ever receives from heaven is the sending to him its disguised and discredited angels.

THE CONSERVATIVE.

A LECTURE DELIVERED AT THE MASONIC TEMPLE, BOSTON,
DECEMBER 9, 1841

THE CONSERVATIVE.

THE two parties which divide the state, the party of Conservatism and that of Innovation, are very old, and have disputed the possession of the world ever since it was made. This quarrel is the subject of civil history. The conservative party established the reverend hierarchies and monarchies of the most ancient world. The battle of patrician and plebeian, of parent state and colony, of old usage and accommodation to new facts, of the rich and the poor, reappears in all countries and times. The war rages not only in battle-fields, in national councils and ecclesiastical synods, but agitates every man's bosom with opposing advantages every hour. On rolls the old world meantime, and now one, now the other gets the day, and still the fight renews itself as if for the first time, under new names and hot personalities.

Such an irreconcilable antagonism of course must have a correspondent depth of seat in the human constitution. It is the opposition of Past and Future, of Memory and Hope, of the Understanding and the Reason.   It is the primal antagonism, the appearance in trifles of the two poles of nature.

There is a fragment of old fable which seems somehow to have been dropped from the current mythologies, which may deserve attention, as it appears to relate to this subject.

Saturn grew weary of sitting alone, or with none but the great Uranus or Heaven beholding him, and he created an oyster.   Then he would act again, but he made nothing more, but went on creating the race of oysters.   Then Uranus cried, ' A new work, O Saturn ! the old is not good again.'

Saturn replied, ' I fear.   There is not only the alternative of making and not making, but also of unmaking.   Seest thou the great sea, how it ebbs and flows? so is it with me ; my power ebbs ; and if I put forth my hands, I shall not do, but undo. Therefore I do what I have done ; I hold what I have got ; and so I resist Night and Chaos.'

' O Saturn,' replied Uranus, 'thou canst not hold thine own but by making more.   Thy oysters are barnacles and cockles, and with the next flowing of the tide they will be pebbles and sea-foam.'

' I see,' rejoins Saturn, 'thou art in league with Night, thou art become an evil eye ; thou spakest from love ; now thy words smite me with hatred.

I appeal to Fate, must there not be rest?' — 'I appeal to Fate also,' said Uranus, 'must there not be motion?' — But Saturn was silent, and went on making oysters for a thousand years.

After that, the word of Uranus came into his mind like a ray of the sun, and he made Jupiter; and then he feared again; and nature froze, the things that were made went backward, and to save the world, Jupiter slew his father Saturn.

This may stand for the earliest account of a conversation on politics between a Conservative and a Radical which has come down to us. It is ever thus. It is the counteraction of the centripetal and the centrifugal forces. Innovation is the salient energy; Conservatism the pause on the last movement. 'That which is was made by God,' saith Conservatism. 'He is leaving that, he is entering this other,' rejoins Innovation.

There is always a certain meanness in the argument of conservatism, joined with a certain superiority in its fact. It affirms because it holds. Its fingers clutch the fact, and it will not open its eyes to see a better fact. The castle which conservatism is set to defend is the actual state of things, good and bad. The project of innovation is the best possible state of things. Of course conservatism always has the worst of the argument, is always apologizing, pleading a necessity, pleading that to

change would be to deteriorate : it must saddle itself with the mountainous load of the violence and
vice of society, must deny the possibility of good,
deny ideas, and suspect and stone the prophet :
whilst innovation is always in the right, triumph-
ant, attacking, and sure of final success.   Conservatism stands on man's confessed limitations, reform on his indisputable infinitude; conservatism
on circumstance, liberalism on power ; one goes to
make an adroit member of the social frame, the
other to postpone all things to the man himself ;
conservatism is debonair and social, reform is individual and imperious.   We are reformers in
spring and summer, in autumn and winter we
stand by the old; reformers in the morning, con-
servers at night.   Reform is affirmative, conservatism negative ; conservatism goes for comfort, reform for truth.   Conservatism is more candid to
behold another's worth ; reform more disposed to
maintain and increase its own.   Conservatism
makes no poetry, breathes no prayer, has no invention ; it is all memory.   Reform has no gratitude,
no prudence, no husbandry.   It makes a great difference to your figure and to your thought whether
your foot is advancing or receding.   Conservatism
never puts the foot forward; in the hour when it
does that, it is not establishment, but reform.   Conservatism tends to universal seeming and treachery,

believes in a negative fate; believes that men's temper governs them; that for me it avails not to trust in principles, they will fail me, I must bend a little; it distrusts nature; it thinks there is a general law without a particular application, — law for all that does not include any one. Reform in its antagonism inclines to asinine resistance, to kick with hoofs; it runs to egotism and bloated self-conceit; it runs to a bodiless pretension, to un-natural refining and elevation which ends in hypocrisy and sensual reaction.

And so, whilst we do not go beyond general statements, it may be safely affirmed of these two metaphysical antagonists, that each is a good half, but an impossible whole. Each exposes the abuses of the other, but in a true society, in a true man, both must combine. Nature does not give the crown of its approbation, namely beauty, to any action or emblem or actor but to one which combines both these elements; not to the rock which resists the waves from age to age, nor to the wave which lashes incessantly the rock, but the superior beauty is with the oak which stands with its hundred arms against the storms of a century, and grows every year like a sapling; or the river which ever flowing, yet is found in the same bed from age to age; or, greatest of all, the man who has subsisted for years amid the changes of nature, yet has distanced himself, so that when you remember what he was, and see what he is, you say, What strides! what a disparity is here!

Throughout nature the past combines in every creature with the present. Each of the convolutions of the sea-shell, each node and spine marks one year of the fish's life; what was the mouth of the shell for one season, with the addition of new matter by the growth of the animal, becoming an ornamental node. The leaves and a shell of soft wood are all that the vegetation of this summer has made; but the solid columnar stem, which lifts that bank of foliage into the air, to draw the eye and to cool us with its shade, is the gift and legacy of dead and buried years.

In nature, each of these elements being always present, each theory has a natural support. As we take our stand on Necessity, or on Ethics, shall we go for the conservative, or for the reformer. If we read the world historically, we shall say, Of all the ages, the present hour and circumstance is the cumulative result; this is the best throw of the dice of nature that has yet been, or that is yet possible. If we see it from the side of Will, or the Moral Sentiment, we shall accuse the Past and the Present, and require the impossible of the Future.

But although this bifold fact lies thus united in real nature, and so united that no man can con-

tinue to exist in whom both these elements do not
work, yet men are not philosophers, but are rather
very foolish children, who, by reason of their partiality, see everything in the most absurd manner,
and are the victims at all times of the nearest object. There is even no philosopher who is a philosopher at all times. Our experience, our perception is conditioned by the need to acquire in parts
and in succession, that is, with every truth a certain falsehood. As this is the invariable method of
our training, we must give it allowance, and suffer
men to learn as they have done for six millenni-
ums, a word at a time; to pair off into insane parties, and learn the amount of truth each knows
by the denial of an equal amount of truth. For
the present, then, to come at what sum is attainable to us, we must even hear the parties plead as
parties.

That which is best about conservatism, that
which, though it cannot be expressed in detail, inspires reverence in all, is the Inevitable. There is
the question not only what the conservative says
for himself, but, why must he say it? What insur-
mountable fact binds him to that side? Here is
the fact which men call Fate, and fate in dread degrees, fate behind fate, not to be disposed of by the
consideration that the Conscience commands this or
that, but necessitating the question whether the fac

ulties of man will play him true in resisting the
facts of universal experience ? For although the
commands of the Conscience are *essentially* absolute, they are *historically* limitary. Wisdom does
not seek a literal rectitude, but an useful, that is
a conditioned one, such a one as the faculties of
man and the constitution of things will warrant.
The reformer, the partisan, loses himself in driving
to the utmost some specialty of right conduct, until
his own nature and all nature resist him ; but Wisdom attempts nothing enormous and dispropor-
tioned to its powers, nothing which it cannot perform or nearly perform. We have all a certain intellection or presentiment of reform existing in the
mind, which does not yet descend into the character, and those who throw themselves blindly on this
lose themselves. Whatever they attempt in that
direction, fails, and reacts suicidally on the actor
himself. This is the penalty of having transcended
nature. For the existing world is not a dream, and
cannot with impunity be treated as a dream ; neither is it a disease ; but it is the ground on which
you stand, it is the mother of whom you were born.
Reform converses with possibilities, perchance with
impossibilities ; but here is sacred fact. This also
was true, or it could not be : it had life in it, or it
could not have existed ; it has life in it, or it could
not continue. Your schemes may be feasible, or

may not be, but this has the endorsement of nature and a long friendship and cohabitation with the powers of nature. This will stand until a better cast of the dice is made. The contest between the Future and the Past is one between Divinity entering and Divinity departing. You are welcome to try your experiments, and, if you can, to displace the actual order by that ideal republic you announce, for nothing but God will expel God. But plainly the burden of proof must lie with the projector. We hold to this, until you can demonstrate something better.

The system of property and law goes back for its origin to barbarous and sacred times ; it is the fruit of the same mysterious cause as the mineral or animal world. There is a natural sentiment and prepossession in favor of age, of ancestors, of barbarous and aboriginal usages, which is a homage to the element of necessity and divinity which is in them. The respect for the old names of places, of mountains and streams, is universal. The Indian and barbarous name can never be supplanted without loss. The ancients tell us that the gods loved the Ethiopians for their stable customs ; and the Egyptians and Chaldeans, whose origin could not be explored, passed among the junior tribes of Greece and Italy for sacred nations.

Moreover, so deep is the foundation of the existing social system, that it leaves no one out of it. We may be partial, but Fate is not. All men have their root in it. You who quarrel with the arrangements of society, and are willing to embroil all, and risk the indisputable good that exists, for the chance of better, live, move, and have your being in this, and your deeds contradict your words every day. For as you cannot jump from the ground without using the resistance of the ground, nor put out the boat to sea without shoving from the shore, nor attain liberty without rejecting obligation, so you are under the necessity of using the Actual order of things, in order to disuse it; to live by it, whilst you wish to take away its life. The past has baked your loaf, and in the strength of its bread you would break up the oven. But you are betrayed by your own nature. You also are conservatives. However men please to style themselves, I see no other than a conservative party. You are not only identical with us in your needs, but also in your methods and aims. You quarrel with my conservatism, but it is to build up one of your own; it will have a new beginning, but the same course and end, the same trials, the same passions; among the lovers of the new I observe that there is a jealousy of the newest, and that the seceder from the seceder is as damnable as the pope himself.

On these and the like grounds of general statement, conservatism plants itself without danger of
being displaced. Especially before this *personal*
appeal, the innovator must confess his weakness,
must confess that no man is to be found good
enough to be entitled to stand champion for the
principle. But when this great tendency comes to
practical encounters, and is challenged by young
men, to whom it is no abstraction, but a fact of
hunger, distress, and exclusion from opportunities,
it must needs seem injurious. The youth, of course,
is an innovator by the fact of his birth. There he
stands, newly born on the planet, a universal beggar, with all the reason of things, one would say,
on his side. In his first consideration how to feed,
clothe, and warm himself, he is met by warnings on
every hand that this thing and that thing have
owners, and he must go elsewhere. Then he says,
'If I am born in the earth, where is my part? have
the goodness, gentlemen of this world, to show me
my wood-lot, where I may fell my wood, my field
where to plant my corn, my pleasant ground where
to build my cabin.'

'Touch any wood, or field, or house-lot, on your
peril,' cry all the gentlemen of this world; 'but
you may come and work in ours, for us, and we
will give you a piece of bread.'

' And what is that peril?'

'Knives and muskets, if we meet you in the act; imprisonment, if we find you afterward.'

'And by what authority, kind gentlemen?'

'By our law.'

'And your law,—is it just?'

'As just for you as it was for us. We wrought for others under this law, and got our lands so.'

'I repeat the question, Is your law just?'

'Not quite just, but necessary. Moreover, it is juster now than it was when we were born; we have made it milder and more equal.'

'I will none of your law,' returns the youth; 'it encumbers me. I cannot understand, or so much as spare time to read that needless library of your laws. Nature has sufficiently provided me with rewards and sharp penalties, to bind me not to transgress. Like the Persian noble of old, I ask " that I may neither command nor obey." I do not wish to enter into your complex social system. I shall serve those whom I can, and they who can will serve me. I shall seek those whom I love, and shun those whom I love not, and what more can all your laws render me?'

With equal earnestness and good faith, replies to this plaintiff an upholder of the establishment, a man of many virtues:

'Your opposition is feather-brained and over-fine. Young man, I have no skill to talk with you, but look at me; I have risen early and sat late, and toiled honestly and painfully for very many years. I never dreamed about methods; I laid my bones to, and drudged for the good I possess; it was not got by fraud, nor by luck, but by work, and you must show me a warrant like these stubborn facts in your own fidelity and labor, before I suffer you, on the faith of a few fine words, to ride into my estate, and claim to scatter it as your own.'

'Now you touch the heart of the matter,' replies the reformer. 'To that fidelity and labor I pay homage. I am unworthy to arraign your manner of living, until I too have been tried. But I should be more unworthy if I did not tell you why I cannot walk in your steps. I find this vast network, which you call property, extended over the whole planet. I cannot occupy the bleakest crag of the White Hills or the Alleghany Range, but some man or corporation steps up to me to show me that it is his. Now, though I am very peaceable, and on my private account could well enough die, since it appears there was some mistake in my creation, and that I have been *mis*sent to this earth, where all the seats were already taken, — yet I feel called upon in behalf of rational nature, which I represent, to declare to you my opinion that if the Earth is yours so also is it mine. All your aggregate existences are less to me a fact than is my own; as I am born to the Earth, so the Earth is given to me, what I want of it to till and to plant; nor could I, without pusillanimity, omit to claim so much. I must not only have a name to live, I must live. My genius leads me to build a different manner of life from any of yours. I cannot then spare you the whole world. I love you better. I must tell you the truth practically; and take that which you call yours. It is God's world and mine; yours as much as you want, mine as much as I want. Besides, I know your ways; I know the symptoms of the disease. To the end of your power you will serve this lie which cheats you. Your want is a gulf which the possession of the broad earth would not fill. Yonder sun in heaven you would pluck down from shining on the universe, and make him a property and privacy, if you could; and the moon and the north star you would quickly have occasion for in your closet and bed-chamber. What you do not want for use, you crave for ornament, and what your convenience could spare, your pride cannot.'

On the other hand, precisely the defence which was set up for the British Constitution, namely that with all its admitted defects, rotten boroughs and monopolies, it worked well, and substantial justice was somehow done; the wisdom and the

worth did get into parliament, and every interest
did by right, or might, or sleight, get represented ;
— the same defence is set up for the existing institutions. They are not the best; they are not just;
and in respect to you, personally, O brave young
man ! they cannot be justified. They have, it is
most true, left you no acre for your own, and no
law but our law, to the ordaining of which you were
no party. But they do answer the end, they are
really friendly to the good, unfriendly to the bad ;
they second the industrious and the kind ; they
foster genius. They really have so much flexibility
as to afford your talent and character, on the whole,
the same chance of demonstration and success
which they might have if there was no law and no
property.

It is trivial and merely superstitious to say that
nothing is given you, no outfit, no exhibition ; for
in this institution of *credit*, which is as universal
as honesty and promise in the human countenance,
always some neighbor stands ready to be bread and
land and tools and stock to the young adventurer.
And if in any one respect they have come short,
see what ample retribution of good they have made.
They have lost no time and spared no expense
to collect libraries, museums, galleries, colleges,
palaces, hospitals, observatories, cities. The ages
have not been idle, nor kings slack, nor the rich nig

gardly. Have we not atoned for this small offence
(which we could not help) of leaving you no right
in the soil, by this splendid indemnity of ancestral
and national wealth? Would you have been born
like a gipsy in a hedge, and preferred your freedom on a heath, and the range of a planet which
had no shed or boscage to cover you from sun and
wind, — to this towered and citied world? to this
world of Rome, and Memphis, and Constantinople,
and Vienna, and Paris, and London, and New
York? For thee Naples, Florence, and Venice;
for thee the fair Mediterranean, the sunny Adri-
atic; for thee both Indies smile; for thee the hospitable North opens its heated palaces under the
polar circle; for thee roads have been cut in every
direction across the land, and fleets of floating palaces with every security for strength and provision
for luxury, swim by sail and by steam through all
the waters of this world. Every island for thee
has a town; every town a hotel. Though thou
wast born landless, yet to thy industry and thrift
and small condescension to the established usage,
— scores of servants are swarming in every strange
place with cap and knee to thy command; scores,
nay hundreds and thousands, for thy wardrobe, thy
table, thy chamber, thy library, thy leisure; and
every whim is anticipated and served by the best
ability of the whole population of each country.

The king on the throne governs for thee, and the judge judges; the barrister pleads, the farmer tills, the joiner hammers, the postman rides. Is it not exaggerating a trifle to insist on a formal acknowledgment of your claims, when these substantial advantages have been secured to you? Now can your children be educated, your labor turned to their advantage, and its fruits secured to them after your death. It is frivolous to say you have no acre, because you have not a mathematically measured piece of land. Providence takes care that you shall have a place, that you are waited for, and come accredited; and as soon as you put your gift to use, you shall have acre or acre's worth according to your exhibition of desert, — acre, if you need land; — acre's worth, if you prefer to draw, or carve, or make shoes or wheels, to the tilling of the soil.

Besides, it might temper your indignation at the supposed wrong which society has done you, to keep the question before you, how society got into this predicament? Who put things on this false basis? No single man, but all men. No man voluntarily and knowingly; but it is the result of that degree of culture there is in the planet. The order of things is as good as the character of the population permits. Consider it as the work of a great and beneficent and progressive necessity, which, from the first pulsation in the first animal

life, up to the present high culture of the best nations, has advanced thus far.   Thank the rude fos-
ter-mother though she has taught you a better wisdom than her own, and has set hopes in your heart
which shall be history in the next ages.   You are
yourself the result of this manner of living, this
foul compromise, this vituperated Sodom.   It nourished you with care and love on its breast, as it had
nourished many a lover of the right and many a
poet, and prophet, and teacher of men.   Is it so ir-
remediably bad ?   Then again, if the mitigations
are considered, do not all the mischiefs virtually
vanish?   The form is bad, but see you not how
every personal character reacts on the form, and
makes it new ?   A strong person makes the law
and custom null before his own will.   Then the
principle of love and truth reappears in the strict-
est courts of fashion and property.   Under the
richest robes, in the darlings of the selectest circles
of European or American aristocracy, the strong
heart will beat with love of mankind, with impatience of accidental distinctions, with the desire to
achieve its own fate and make every ornament it
wears authentic and real.

Moreover, as we have already shown that there
is no pure reformer, so it is to be considered that
there is no pure conservative, no man who from
the beginning to the end of his life maintains the

defective institutions; but he who sets his face like a flint against every novelty, when approached in the confidence of conversation, in the presence of friendly and generous persons, has also his gracious and relenting moments, and espouses for the time the cause of man; and even if this be a shortlived emotion, yet the remembrance of it in private hours mitigates his selfishness and compliance with custom.

The Friar Bernard lamented in his cell on Mount Cenis the crimes of mankind, and rising one morning before day from his bed of moss and dry leaves, he gnawed his roots and berries, drank of the spring, and set forth to go to Rome to reform the corruption of mankind. On his way he encountered many travellers who greeted him courteously, and the cabins of the peasants and the castles of the lords supplied his few wants. When he came at last to Rome, his piety and good will easily introduced him to many families of the rich, and on the first day he saw and talked with gentle mothers with their babes at their breasts, who told him how much love they bore their children, and how they were perplexed in their daily walk lest they should fail in their duty to them. ' What! ' he said, ' and this on rich embroidered carpets, on marble floors, with cunning sculpture, and carved wood, and rich pictures, and piles of books about you ? ' — ' Look at our pictures and books,' they said, ' and we will tell you, good Father, how we spent the last evening. These are stories of godly children and holy families and romantic sacrifices made in old or in recent times by great and not mean persons ; and last evening our family was collected and our husbands and brothers discoursed sadly on what we could save and give in the hard times.' Then came in the men, and they said, ' What cheer, brother ? Does thy convent want gifts ? ' Then the friar Bernard went home swiftly with other thoughts than he brought, saying, ' This way of life is wrong, yet these Romans, whom I prayed God to destroy, are lovers, they are lovers ; what can I do ? '

The reformer concedes that these mitigations exist, and that if he proposed comfort, he should take sides with the establishment. Your words are excellent, but they do not tell the whole. Conservatism is affluent and openhanded, but there is a cunning juggle in riches. I observe that they take somewhat for everything they give. I look bigger, but am less ; I have more clothes, but am not so warm ; more armor, but less courage ; more books, but less wit. What you say of your planted, builded and decorated world is true enough, and I gladly avail myself of its convenience ; yet I have remarked that what holds in particular, holds in general, that the plant Man does not require for his most glorious flowering this pomp of preparation and convenience, but the thoughts of some beggarly Homer who strolled, God knows when, in the infancy and barbarism of the old world ; the gravity and sense of some slave Moses who leads away his fellow slaves from their masters ; the contemplation of some Scythian Anacharsis ; the erect, formidable valor of some Dorian townsmen in the town of Sparta ; the vigor of Clovis the Frank, and Alfred the Saxon, and Alaric the Goth, and Mahomet, Ali and Omar the Arabians, Saladin the Curd, and Othman the Turk, sufficed to build what you call society on the spot and in the instant when the sound mind in a sound body appeared. Rich and fine is your dress, O conservatism ! your horses are of the best blood ; your roads are well cut and well paved ; your pantry is full of meats and your cellar of wines, and a very good state and condition are you for gentlemen and ladies to live under ; but every one of these goods steals away a drop of my blood. I want the necessity of supplying my own wants. All this costly culture of yours is not necessary. Greatness does not need it. Yonder peasant, who sits neglected there in a corner, carries a whole revolution of man and nature in his head, which shall be a sacred history to some future ages. For man is the end of nature ; nothing so easily organizes itself in every part of the universe as he ; no moss, no lichen is so easily born ; and he takes along with him and puts out from himself the whole apparatus of society and condition *extempore*, as an army encamps in a desert, and where all was just now blowing sand, creates a white city in an hour, a government, a market, a place for feasting, for conversation, and for love.

These considerations, urged by those whose characters and whose fortunes are yet to be formed, must needs command the sympathy of all reasonable persons. But beside that charity which should make all adult persons interested for the youth, and engage them to see that he has a free field and fair play on his entrance into life, we are bound to see that the society of which we compose a part, does not permit the formation or continuance of views and practices injurious to the honor and welfare of mankind. The objection to conservatism, when embodied in a party, is that in its love of acts it hates principles ; it lives in the senses, not in truth ; it sacrifices to despair ; it goes for availableness in its candidate, not for worth ; and for expediency in its measures, and not for the right. Under pretence of allowing for friction, it makes so many additions and supplements to the machine of society that it will play smoothly and softly, but will no longer grind any grist.

The conservative party in the universe concedes
that the radical would talk sufficiently to the purpose, if we were still in the garden of Eden; he
legislates for man as he ought to be; his theory is
right, but he makes no allowance for friction; and
this omission makes his whole doctrine false. The
idealist retorts that the conservative falls into a far
more noxious error in the other extreme. The conservative assumes sickness as a necessity, and his
social frame is a hospital, his total legislation is for
the present distress, a universe in slippers and flan-
nels, with bib and papspoon, swallowing pills and
herb-tea. Sickness gets organized as well as health,
the vice as well as the virtue. Now that a vicious
system of trade has existed so long, it has stereo-
typed itself in the human generation, and misers
are born. And now that sickness has got such a
foothold, leprosy has grown cunning, has got into
the ballot-box; the lepers outvote the clean; society has resolved itself into a Hospital Committee,
and all its laws are quarantine. If any man resist
and set up a foolish hope he has entertained as
good against the general despair, Society frowns on
him, shuts him out of her opportunities, her grana-
ries, her refectories, her water and bread, and will
serve him a sexton's turn. Conservatism takes as
low a view of every part of human action and passion. Its religion is just as bad; a lozenge for the

sick; a dolorous tune to beguile the distemper; mitigations of pain by pillows and anodynes; always mitigations, never remedies; pardons for sin, funeral honors, — never self-help, renovation, and virtue. Its social and political action has no better aim ; to keep out wind and weather, to bring the week and year about, and make the world last our day ; not to sit on the world and steer it ; not to sink the memory of the past in the glory of a new and more excellent creation ; a timid cobbler and patcher, it degrades whatever it touches. The cause of education is urged in this country with the utmost earnestness, — on what ground? Why on this, that the people have the power, and if they are not instructed to sympathize with the intelligent, reading, trading, and governing class; inspired with a taste for the same competitions and prizes, they will upset the fair pageant of Judicature, and perhaps lay a hand on the sacred muniments of wealth itself, and new distribute the land. Religion is taught in the same spirit. The contractors who were building a road out of Baltimore, some years ago, found the Irish laborers quarrelsome and refractory to a degree that embarrassed the agents and seriously interrupted the progress of the work. The corporation were advised to call off the police and build a Catholic chapel, which they did; the priest presently restored order, and the work went on prosperously. Such hints, be sure, are too valuable to be lost. If you do not value the Sabbath, or other religious institutions, give yourself no concern about maintaining them. They have already acquired a market value as conservators of property; and if priest and church-member should fail, the chambers of commerce and the presidents of the banks, the very innholders and landlords of the county, would muster with fury to their support.

Of course, religion in such hands loses its essence. Instead of that reliance which the soul suggests, on the eternity of truth and duty, men are misled into a reliance on institutions, which, the moment they cease to be the instantaneous creations of the devout sentiment, are worthless. Religion among the low becomes low. As it loses its truth, it loses credit with the sagacious. They detect the falsehood of the preaching, but when they say so, all good citizens cry, Hush; do not weaken the State, do not take off the strait jacket from dangerous persons. Every honest fellow must keep up the hoax the best he can; must patronize providence and piety, and wherever he sees anything that will keep men amused, schools or churches or poetry or picture-galleries or music, or what not, he must cry "Hist-a-boy," and urge the game on. What a compliment we pay to the good SPIRIT with our superserviceable zeal!

But not to balance reasons for and against the establishment any longer, and if it still be asked in this necessity of partial organization, which party on the whole has the highest claims on our sympathy, — I bring it home to the private heart, where all such questions must have their final arbitrement. How will every strong and generous mind choose its ground, — with the defenders of the old? or with the seekers of the new? Which is that state which promises to edify a great, brave, and beneficent man; to throw him on his resources, and tax the strength of his character? On which part will each of us find himself in the hour of health and of aspiration?

I understand well the respect of mankind for war, because that breaks up the Chinese stagnation of society, and demonstrates the personal merits of all men. A state of war or anarchy, in which law has little force, is so far valuable that it puts every man on trial. The man of principle is known as such, and even in the fury of faction is respected. In the civil wars of France, Montaigne alone, among all the French gentry, kept his castle gates unbarred, and made his personal integrity as good at least as a regiment. The man of courage and resources is shown, and the effeminate and base person. Those who rise above war, and those who fall below it, it easily discriminates, as well as those who, accepting its rude conditions, keep their own head by their own sword.

But in peace and a commercial state we depend, not as we ought, on our knowledge and all men's knowledge that we are honest men, but we cowardly lean on the virtue of others. For it is always at last the virtue of some men in the society, which keeps the law in any reverence and power. Is there not something shameful that I should owe my peaceful occupancy of my house and field, not to the knowledge of my countrymen that I am useful, but to their respect for sundry other reputable persons, I know not whom, whose joint virtue still keeps the law in good odor?

It will never make any difference to a hero what the laws are. His greatness will shine and accomplish itself unto the end, whether they second him or not. If he have earned his bread by drudgery, and in the narrow and crooked ways which were all an evil law had left him, he will make it at least honorable by his expenditure. Of the past he will take no heed; for its wrongs he will not hold himself responsible: he will say, All the meanness of my progenitors shall not bereave me of the power to make this hour and company fair and fortunate. Whatsoever streams of power and commodity flow to me, shall of me acquire healing virtue, and become fountains of safety. Cannot I too

descend a Redeemer into nature? Whosover hereafter shall name my name, shall not record a male-
factor but a benefactor in the earth. If there be
power in good intention, in fidelity, and in toil, the
north wind shall be purer, the stars in heaven shall
glow with a kindlier beam, that I have lived. I
am primarily engaged to myself to be a public servant of all the gods, to demonstrate to all men that
there is intelligence and good will at the heart of
things, and ever higher and yet higher leadings.
These are my engagements; how can your law
further or hinder me in what I shall do to men?
On the other hand, these dispositions establish
their relations to me. Wherever there is worth, I
shall be greeted. Wherever there are men, are
the objects of my study and love. Sooner or later
all men will be my friends, and will testify in all
methods the energy of their regard. I cannot
thank your law for my protection. I protect it.
It is not in its power to protect me. It is my business to make myself revered. I depend on my
honor, my labor, and my dispositions for my place
in the affections of mankind, and not on any conventions or parchments of yours.

But if I allow myself in derelictions and become
idle and dissolute, I quickly come to love the protection of a strong law, because I feel no title in
myself to my advantages. To the intemperate and

covetous person no love flows; to him mankind
would pay no rent, no dividend, if force were once
relaxed; nay, if they could give their verdict, they
would say that his self-indulgence and his oppression deserved punishment from society, and not
that rich board and lodging he now enjoys. The
law acts then as a screen of his unworthiness, and
makes him worse the longer it protects him.

In conclusion, to return from this alternation of
partial views to the high platform of universal and
necessary history, it is a happiness for mankind
that innovation has got on so far and has so free a
field before it. The boldness of the hope men entertain transcends all former experience. It calms
and cheers them with the picture of a simple and
equal life of truth and piety. And this hope flow-
ered on what tree? It was not imported from the
stock of some celestial plant, but grew here on the
wild crab of conservatism. It is much that this
old and vituperated system of things has borne so
fair a child. It predicts that amidst a planet peo-
pled with conservatives, one Reformer may yet be
born.

THE TRANSCENDENTALIST.

A LECTURE READ AT THE MASONIC TEMPLE, BOSTON, JANUARY,
1842.

THE TRANSCENDENTALIST.

———◆———

THE first thing we have to say respecting what are called *new views* here in New England, at the present time, is, that they are not new, but the very oldest of thoughts cast into the mould of these new times. The light is always identical in its composition, but it falls on a great variety of objects, and by so falling is first revealed to us, not in its own form, for it is formless, but in theirs; in like manner, thought only appears in the objects it classifies. What is popularly called Transcendentalism among us, is Idealism; Idealism as it appears in 1842. As thinkers, mankind have ever divided into two sects, Materialists and Idealists; the first class founding on experience, the second on consciousness; the first class beginning to think from the data of the senses, the second class perceive that the senses are not final, and say, The senses give us representations of things, but what are the things themselves, they cannot tell. The materialist insists on facts, on history, on the force of circumstances and the animal wants of man; the

idealist on the power of Thought and of Will, on inspiration, on miracle, on individual culture. These
two modes of thinking are both natural, but the
idealist contends that his way of thinking is in
higher nature. He concedes all that the other affirms, admits the impressions of sense, admits their
cohèrency, their use and beauty, and then asks the
materialist for his grounds of assurance that things
are as his senses represent them. But I, he says,
affirm facts not affected by the illusions of sense,
facts which are of the same nature as the faculty
which reports them, and not liable to doubt ; facts
which in their first appearance to us assume a native superiority to material facts, degrading these
into a language by which the first are to be spoken ;
facts which it only needs a retirement from the
senses to discern. Every materialist will be an
idealist ; but an idealist can never go backward to
be a materialist.

The idealist, in speaking of events, sees them as
spirits. He does not deny the sensuous fact : by
no means ; but he will not see that alone. He does
not deny the presence of this table, this chair, and
the walls of this room, but he looks at these things
as the reverse side of the tapestry, as the *other end*,
each being a sequel or completion of a spiritual
fact which nearly concerns him. This manner of
looking at things transfers every object in nature

from an independent and anomalous position without there, into the consciousness. Even the materialist Condillac, perhaps the most logical expounder
of materialism, was constrained to say, " Though
we should soar into the heavens, though we should
sink into the abyss, we never go out of ourselves;
it is always our own thought that we perceive."
What more could an idealist say?

The materialist, secure in the certainty of sensa-
tion, mocks at fine-spun theories, at star-gazers and
dreamers, and believes that his life is solid, that he
at least takes nothing for granted, but knows where
he stands, and what he does. Yet how easy it is
to show him that he also is a phantom walking and
working amid phantoms, and that he need only ask
a question or two beyond his daily questions to
find his solid universe growing dim and impalpable
before his sense. The sturdy capitalist, no matter
how deep and square on blocks of Quincy granite
he lays the foundations of his banking-house or
Exchange, must set it, at last, not on a cube cor-
responding to the angles of his structure, but on a
mass of unknown materials and solidity, red-hot or
white-hot perhaps at the core, which rounds off to
an almost perfect sphericity, and lies floating in soft
air, and goes spinning away, dragging bank and
banker with it at a rate of thousands of miles the
hour, he knows not whither, — a bit of bullet, now

glimmering, now darkling through a small cubic space on the edge of an unimaginable pit of emptiness. And this wild balloon, in which his whole venture is embarked, is a just symbol of his whole state and faculty. One thing at least, he says, is certain, and does not give me the headache, that figures do not lie; the multiplication table has been hitherto found unimpeachable truth; and, moreover, if I put a gold eagle in my safe, I find it again to-morrow; — but for these thoughts, I know not whence they are. They change and pass away. But ask him why he believes that an uniform experience will continue uniform, or on what grounds he founds his faith in his figures, and he will perceive that his mental fabric is built up on just as strange and quaking foundations as his proud edifice of stone.

In the order of thought, the materialist takes his departure from the external world, and esteems a man as one product of that. The idealist takes his departure from his consciousness, and reckons the world an appearance. The materialist respects sensible masses, Society, Government, social art and luxury, every establishment, every mass, whether majority of numbers, or extent of space, or amount of objects, every social action. The idealist has another measure, which is metaphysical, namely the *rank* which things themselves take in his consciousness; not at all the size or appearance. Mind is the only reality, of which men and all other natures are better or worse reflectors. Nature, literature, history, are only subjective phenomena. Although in his action overpowered by the laws of action, and so, warmly coöperating with men, even preferring them to himself, yet when he speaks scientifically, or after the order of thought, he is constrained to degrade persons into representatives of truths. He does not respect labor, or the products of labor, namely property, otherwise than as a manifold symbol, illustrating with wonderful fidelity of details the laws of being; he does not respect government, except as far as it reiterates the law of his mind; nor the church, nor charities, nor arts, for themselves; but hears, as at a vast distance, what they say, as if his consciousness would speak to him through a pantomimic scene. His thought, — that is the Universe. His experience inclines him to behold the procession of facts you call the world, as flowing perpetually outward from an invisible, unsounded centre in himself, centre alike of him and of them, and necessitating him to regard all things as having a subjective or relative existence, relative to that aforesaid Unknown Centre of him.

From this transfer of the world into the consciousness, this beholding of all things in the mind, follow easily his whole ethics. It is simpler to be self-dependent. The height, the deity of man is to be self-sustained, to need no gift, no foreign force. Society is good when it does not violate me, but best when it is likest to solitude. Everything real is self-existent. Everything divine shares the self-existence of Deity. All that you call the world is the shadow of that substance which you are, the perpetual creation of the powers of thought, of those that are dependent and of those that are independent of your will. Do not cumber yourself with fruitless pains to mend and remedy remote effects ; let the soul be erect, and all things will go well. You think me the child of my circumstances : I make my circumstance. Let any thought or motive of mine be different from that they are, the difference will transform my condition and economy. I — this thought which is called I — is the mould into which the world is poured like melted wax. The mould is invisible, but the world betrays the shape of the mould. You call it the power of circumstance, but it is the power of me. Am I in harmony with myself ? my position will seem to you just and commanding. Am I vicious and insane ? my fortunes will seem to you obscure and descending. As I am, so shall I associate, and so shall I act ; Cæsar's history will paint out Cæsar. Jesus acted so, because he thought so. I do not wish to overlook or to gainsay any reality; I say I make my circumstance; but if you ask me, Whence am I? I feel like other men my relation to that Fact which cannot be spoken, or defined, nor even thought, but which exists, and will exist.

The Transcendentalist adopts the whole connection of spiritual doctrine. He believes in miracle, in the perpetual openness of the human mind to new influx of light and power; he believes in inspiration, and in ecstasy. He wishes that the spiritual principle should be suffered to demonstrate itself to the end, in all possible applications to the state of man, without the admission of anything unspiritual; that is, anything positive, dogmatic, personal. Thus the spiritual measure of inspiration is the depth of the thought, and never, who said it? And so he resists all attempts to palm other rules and measures on the spirit than its own.

In action he easily incurs the charge of antinomianism by his avowal that he, who has the Lawgiver, may with safety not only neglect, but even contravene every written commandment. In the play of Othello, the expiring Desdemona absolves her husband of the murder, to her attendant Emilia. Afterwards, when Emilia charges him with the crime, Othello exclaims,

" You heard her say herself it was not I."

Emilia replies,

" The more angel she, and thou the blacker devil."

Of this fine incident, Jacobi, the Transcendental moralist, makes use, with other parallel instances, in his reply to Fichte.   Jacobi, refusing all meas-ure of right and wrong except the determinations of the private spirit, remarks that there is no crime but has sometimes been a virtue.   " I," he says, " am that atheist, that godless person who, in op-position to an imaginary doctrine of calculation, would lie as the dying Desdemona lied ; would lie and deceive, as Pylades when he personated Ores-tes ; would assassinate like Timoleon ; would per-jure myself like Epaminondas and John de Witt ; I would resolve on suicide like Cato ; I would com-mit sacrilege with David ; yea, and pluck ears of corn on the Sabbath, for no other reason than that I was fainting for lack of food.   For I have assur-ance in myself that in pardoning these faults ac-cording to the letter, man exerts the sovereign right which the majesty of his being confers on him ; he sets the seal of his divine nature to the grace he ac-cords." [1]

In like manner, if there is anything grand and daring in human thought or virtue, any reliance on the vast, the unknown ; any presentiment, any ex-travagance of faith, the spiritualist adopts it as most in nature.   The oriental mind has always

[1] Coleridge's Translation.

tended to this largeness. Buddhism is an expression of it. The Buddhist, who thanks no man, who says "Do not flatter your benefactors," but who, in his conviction that every good deed can by no possibility escape its reward, will not deceive the benefactor by pretending that he has done more than he should, is a Transcendentalist.

You will see by this sketch that there is no such thing as a Transcendental *party* ; that there is no pure Transcendentalist ; that we know of none but prophets and heralds of such a philosophy ; that all who by strong bias of nature have leaned to the spiritual side in doctrine, have stopped short of their goal. We have had many harbingers and forerunners ; but of a purely spiritual life, history has afforded no example. I mean we have yet no man who has leaned entirely on his character, and eaten angels' food ; who, trusting to his sentiments, found life made of miracles ; who, working for universal aims, found himself fed, he knew not how ; clothed, sheltered, and weaponed, he knew not how, and yet it was done by his own hands. Only in the instinct of the lower animals we find the suggestion of the methods of it, and something higher than our understanding. The squirrel hoards nuts and the bee gathers honey, without knowing what they do, and they are thus provided for without selfishness or disgrace.

Shall we say then that Transcendentalism is the Saturnalia or excess of Faith ; the presentiment of a faith proper to man in his integrity, excessive only when his imperfect obedience hinders the satisfaction of his wish ?   Nature is transcendental, exists primarily, necessarily, ever works and advances, yet takes no thought for the morrow.   Man owns the dignity of the life which throbs around him, in chemistry, and tree, and animal, and in the involuntary functions of his own body ; yet he is balked when he tries to fling himself into this enchanted circle, where all is done without degradation.   Yet genius and virtue predict in man the same absence of private ends and of condescension to circumstances, united with every trait and talent of beauty and power.

This way of thinking, falling on Roman times, made Stoic philosophers ; falling on despotic times, made patriot Catos and Brutuses ; falling on superstitious times, made prophets and apostles ; on popish times, made protestants and ascetic monks, preachers of Faith against the preachers of Works ; on prelatical times, made Puritans and Quakers ; and falling on Unitarian and commercial times, makes the peculiar shades of Idealism which we know.

It is well known to most of my audience that the Idealism of the present day acquired the name of

Transcendental from the use of that term by Immanuel Kant, of Konigsberg, who replied to the skeptical philosophy of Locke, which insisted that there was nothing in the intellect which was not previously in the experience of the senses, by showing that there was a very important class of ideas or imperative forms, which did not come by experience, but through which experience was acquired; that these were intuitions of the mind itself; and he denominated them *Transcendental* forms. The extraordinary profoundness and precision of that man's thinking have given vogue to his nomenclature, in Europe and America, to that extent that whatever belongs to the class of intuitive thought is popularly called at the present day *Transcendental*.

Although, as we have said, there is no pure Transcendentalist, yet the tendency to respect the intuitions and to give them, at least in our creed, all authority over our experience, has deeply colored the conversation and poetry of the present day; and the history of genius and of religion in these times, though impure, and as yet not incarnated in any powerful individual, will be the history of this tendency.

It is a sign of our times, conspicuous to the coarsest observer, that many intelligent and religious persons withdraw themselves from the common labors and competitions of the market and the caucus, and betake themselves to a certain solitary and critical way of living, from which no solid fruit has yet appeared to justify their separation. They hold themselves aloof: they feel the disproportion between their faculties and the work offered them, and they prefer to ramble in the country and perish of ennui, to the degradation of such charities and such ambitions as the city can propose to them. They are striking work, and crying out for somewhat worthy to do! What they do is done only because they are overpowered by the humanities that speak on all sides; and they consent to such labor as is open to them, though to their lofty dream the writing of Iliads or Hamlets, or the building of cities or empires seems drudgery.

Now every one must do after his kind, be he asp or angel, and these must. The question which a wise man and a student of modern history will ask, is, what that kind is? And truly, as in ecclesiastical history we take so much pains to know what the Gnostics, what the Essenes, what the Manichees, and what the Reformers believed, it would not misbecome us to inquire nearer home, what these companions and contemporaries of ours think and do, at least so far as these thoughts and actions appear to be not accidental and personal, but com-

mon to many, and the inevitable flower of the Tree
of Time. Our American literature and spiritual
history are, we confess, in the optative mood; but
whoso knows these seething brains, these admirable
radicals, these unsocial worshippers, these talkers
who talk the sun and moon away, will believe that
this heresy cannot pass away without leaving its
mark.

They are lonely; the spirit of their writing and
conversation is lonely; they repel influences; they
shun general society; they incline to shut themselves in their chamber in the house, to live in the
country rather than in the town, and to find their
tasks and amusements in solitude. Society, to be
sure, does not like this very well; it saith, Whoso
goes to walk alone, accuses the whole world; he
declares all to be unfit to be his companions; it is
very uncivil, nay, insulting; Society will retaliate.
Meantime, this retirement does not proceed from
any whim on the part of these separators; but if
any one will take pains to talk with them, he will
find that this part is chosen both from temperament
and from principle; with some unwillingness too,
and as a choice of the less of two evils; for these
persons are not by nature melancholy, sour, and
unsocial, — they are not stockish or brute, — but
joyous, susceptible, affectionate; they have even
more than others a great wish to be loved. Like

the young Mozart, they are rather ready to cry ten
times a day, " But are you sure you love me? "
Nay, if they tell you their whole thought, they will
own that love seems to them the last and highest
gift of nature ; that there are persons whom in
their hearts they daily thank for existing, — persons whose faces are perhaps unknown to them, but
whose fame and spirit have penetrated their solitude, — and for whose sake they wish to exist.   To
behold the beauty of another character, which inspires a new interest in our own ; to behold the
beauty lodged in a human being, with such vivacity
of apprehension that I am instantly forced home
to inquire if I am not deformity itself ; to behold
in another the expression of a love so high that it
assures itself, — assures itself also to me against
every possible casualty except my unworthiness ;
— these are degrees on the scale of human happiness to which they have ascended ; and it is a fidelity to this sentiment which has made common association distasteful to them.   They wish a just
and even fellowship, or none.   They cannot gossip
with you, and they do not wish, as they are sincere
and religious, to gratify any mere curiosity which
you may entertain.   Like fairies, they do not wish
to be spoken of.   Love me, they say, but do not
ask who is my cousin and my uncle.   If you do
not need to hear my thought, because you can read

it in my face and behavior, then I will tell it you
from sunrise to sunset. If you cannot divine it,
you would not understand what I say. I will not
molest myself for you. I do not wish to be profaned.

And yet, it seems as if this loneliness, and not
this love, would prevail in their circumstances, because of the extravagant demand they make on
human nature. That, indeed, constitutes a new
feature in their portrait, that they are the most exacting and extortionate critics. Their quarrel with
every man they meet is not with his kind, but with
his degree. There is not enough of him, — that is
the only fault. They prolong their privilege of
childhood in this wise; of doing nothing, but making immense demands on all the gladiators in the
lists of action and fame. They make us feel the
strange disappointment which overcasts every human youth. So many promising youths, and never
a finished man! The profound nature will have a
savage rudeness; the delicate one will be shallow,
or the victim of sensibility; the richly accomplished
will have some capital absurdity; and so every
piece has a crack. 'T is strange, but this master-
piece is the result of such an extreme delicacy that
the most unobserved flaw in the boy will neutralize
the most aspiring genius, and spoil the work. Talk
with a seaman of the hazards to life in his profession

and he will ask you, 'Where are the old sailors?
Do you not see that all are young men?' And we,
on this sea of human thought, in like manner inquire, Where are the old idealists? where are they
who represented to the last generation that extravagant hope which a few happy aspirants suggest to
ours? In looking at the class of counsel, and
power, and wealth, and at the matronage of the
land, amidst all the prudence and all the triviality,
one asks, Where are they who represented genius,
virtue, the invisible and heavenly world, to these?
Are they dead, — taken in early ripeness to the
gods, — as ancient wisdom foretold their fate? Or
did the high idea die out of them, and leave their
unperfumed body as its tomb and tablet, announcing to all that the celestial inhabitant, who once
gave them beauty, had departed? Will it be better with the new generation? We easily predict a
fair future to each new candidate who enters the
lists, but we are frivolous and volatile, and by low
aims and ill example do what we can to defeat this
hope. Then these youths bring us a rough but ef-
fectual aid. By their unconcealed dissatisfaction
they expose our poverty and the insignificance of
man to man. A man is a poor limitary benefactor.
He ought to be a shower of benefits — a great influence, which should never let his brother go, but
should refresh old merits continually with new ones;

so that though absent he should never be out of my mind, his name never far from my lips; but if the earth should open at my side, or my last hour were come, his name should be the prayer I should utter to the Universe. But in our experience, man is cheap and friendship wants its deep sense. We affect to dwell with our friends in their absence, but we do not; when deed, word, or letter comes not, they let us go. These exacting children advertise us of our wants. There is no compliment, no smooth speech with them; they pay you only this one compliment, of insatiable expectation; they aspire, they severely exact, and if they only stand fast in this watch-tower, and persist in demanding unto the end, and without end, then are they terrible friends, whereof poet and priest cannot choose but stand in awe; and what if they eat clouds, and drink wind, they have not been without service to the race of man.

With this passion for what is great and extraordinary, it cannot be wondered at that they are repelled by vulgarity and frivolity in people. They say to themselves, It is better to be alone than in bad company. And it is really a wish to be met, — the wish to find society for their hope and religion, — which prompts them to shun what is called society. They feel that they are never so fit for friendship as when they have quitted mankind and taken themselves to friend. A picture, a book, a favorite spot in the hills or the woods which they can people with the fair and worthy creation of the fancy, can give them often forms so vivid that these for the time shall seem real, and society the illu sion.

But their solitary and fastidious manners not only withdraw them from the conversation, but from the labors of the world ; they are not good citizens, not good members of society ; unwillingly they bear their part of the public and private bur- dens; they do not willingly share in the public charities, in the public religious rites, in the enter- prises of education, of missions foreign and domes- tic, in the abolition of the slave - trade, or in the temperance society. They do not even like to vote. The philanthropists inquire whether Transcenden- talism does not mean sloth: they had as lief hear that their friend is dead, as that he is a Transcen- dentalist ; for then is he paralyzed, and can never do anything for humanity. What right, cries the good world, has the man of genius to retreat from work, and indulge himself ? The popular literary creed seems to be, ' I am a sublime genius ; I ought not therefore to labor.' But genius is the power to labor better and more availably. Deserve thy genius : exalt it. The good, the illuminated, sit apart from the rest, censuring their dulness and vices, as if they thought that by sitting very grand in their chairs, the very brokers, attorneys, and congressmen would see the error of their ways, and flock to them. But the good and wise must learn to act, and carry salvation to the combatants and demagogues in the dusty arena below.

On the part of these children it is replied that life and their faculty seem to them gifts too rich to be squandered on such trifles as you propose to them. What you call your fundamental institutions, your great and holy causes, seem to them great abuses, and, when nearly seen, paltry matters. Each 'cause' as it is called, — say Abolition, Temperance, say Calvinism, or Unitarianism, — becomes speedily a little shop, where the article, let it have been at first never so subtle and ethereal, is now made up into portable and convenient cakes, and retailed in small quantities to suit purchasers. You make very free use of these words 'great' and 'holy,' but few things appear to them such. Few persons have any magnificence of nature to inspire enthusiasm, and the philanthropies and charities have a certain air of quackery. As to the general course of living, and the daily employments of men, they cannot see much virtue in these, since they are parts of this vicious circle ; and as no great ends are answered by the men, there is nothing noble in the arts by which they are maintained. Nay, they have made the experiment and found that from the liberal professions to the coarsest manual labor, and from the courtesies of the academy and the college to the conventions of the cotillon-room and the morning call, there is a spirit of cowardly compromise and seeming which intimates a frightful skepticism, a life without love, and an activity without an aim.

Unless the action is necessary, unless it is adequate, I do not wish to perform it. I do not wish to do one thing but once. I do not love routine. Once possessed of the principle, it is equally easy to make four or forty thousand applications of it. A great man will be content to have indicated in any the slightest manner his perception of the reigning Idea of his time, and will leave to those who like it the multiplication of examples. When he has hit the white, the rest may shatter the target. Every thing admonishes us how needlessly long life is. Every moment of a hero so raises and cheers us that a twelvemonth is an age. All that the brave Xanthus brings home from his wars is the recollection that at the storming of Samos, " in the heat of the battle, Pericles smiled on me, and passed on to another detachment." It is the quality of the moment, not the number of days, of events, or of actors, that imports.

New, we confess, and by no means happy, is our condition: if you want the aid of our labor, we ourselves stand in greater want of the labor. We are miserable with inaction. We perish of rest and rust : but we do not like your work.

'Then,' says the world, 'show me your own.'

'We have none.'

'What will you do, then?' cries the world.

'We will wait.'

'How long?'

'Until the Universe beckons and calls us to work.'

'But whilst you wait, you grow old and useless.'

'Be it so : I can sit in a corner and *perish* (as you call it), but I will not move until I have the highest command. If no call should come for years, for centuries, then I know that the want of the Universe is the attestation of faith by my abstinence. Your virtuous projects, so called, do not cheer me. I know that which shall come will cheer me. If I cannot work at least I need not lie. All that is clearly due to-day is not to lie. In other places other men have encountered sharp trials, and have behaved themselves well. The martyrs were sawn asunder, or hung alive on meat-hooks. Cannot we screw our courage to patience and truth, and without complaint, or even with good-humor, await our turn of action in the Infinite Counsels?'

But to come a little closer to the secret of these

persons, we must say that to them it seems a very easy matter to answer the objections of the man of the world, but not so easy to dispose of the doubts and objections that occur to themselves. They are exercised in their own spirit with queries which acquaint them with all adversity, and with the trials of the bravest heroes. When I asked them concerning their private experience, they answered somewhat in this wise: It is not to be denied that there must be some wide difference between my faith and other faith; and mine is a certain brief experience, which surprised me in the highway or in the market, in some place, at some time, — whether in the body or out of the body, God knoweth, — and made me aware that I had played the fool with fools all this time, but that law existed for me and for all; that to me belonged trust, a child's trust and obedience, and the worship of ideas, and I should never be fool more. Well, in the space of an hour probably, I was let down from this height; I was at my old tricks, the selfish member of a selfish society. My life is superficial, takes no root in the deep world; I ask, When shall I die and be relieved of the responsibility of seeing an Universe which I do not use? I wish to exchange this flash-of-lightning faith for continuous daylight, this fever-glow for a benign climate.

These two states of thought diverge every mo

ment, and stand in wild contrast. To him who looks at his life from these moments of illumination, it will seem that he skulks and plays a mean, shiftless and subaltern part in the world. That is to be done which he has not skill to do, or to be said which others can say better, and he lies by, or occupies his hands with some plaything, until his hour comes again. Much of our reading, much of our labor, seems mere waiting : it was not that we were born for. Any other could do it as well or better. So little skill enters into these works, so little do they mix with the divine life, that it really signifies little what we do, whether we turn a grindstone, or ride, or run, or make fortunes, or govern the state. The worst feature of this double consciousness is, that the two lives, of the understanding and of the soul, which we lead, really show very little relation to each other ; never meet and measure each other : one prevails now, all buzz and din ; and the other prevails then, all infinitude and paradise ; and, with the progress of life, the two discover no greater disposition to reconcile themselves. Yet, what is my faith ? What am I ? What but a thought of serenity and independence, an abode in the deep blue sky ? Presently the clouds shut down again ; yet we retain the belief that this petty web we weave will at last be overshot and reticulated with veins of the blue, and that the moments will characterize the days.   Patience, then, is for us, is it not?   Patience, and still patience.   When we pass, as presently we shall, into some new infinitude, out of this Iceland of negations, it will please us to reflect that though we had few virtues or consolations, we bore with our indigence, nor once strove to repair it with hypocrisy or false heat of any kind.

But this class are not sufficiently characterized if we omit to add that they are lovers and worshippers of Beauty.   In the eternal trinity of Truth, Goodness, and Beauty, each in its perfection including the three, they prefer to make Beauty the sign and head.   Something of the same taste is observable in all the moral movements of the time, in the religious and benevolent enterprises.   They have a liberal, even an æsthetic spirit.   A reference to Beauty in action sounds to be sure a little hollow and ridiculous in the ears of the old church.   In politics, it has often sufficed, when they treated of justice, if they kept the bounds of selfish calculation.   If they granted restitution, it was prudence which granted it.   But the justice which is now claimed for the black, and the pauper, and the drunkard, is for Beauty, — is for a necessity to the soul of the agent, not of the beneficiary.   I say this is the tendency, not yet the realization.   Our virtue totters and trips, does not yet walk firmly.   Its representatives are austere; they preach and denounce; their rectitude is not yet a grace. They are still liable to that slight taint of burlesque which in our strange world attaches to the zealot. A saint should be as dear as the apple of the eye. Yet we are tempted to smile, and we flee from the working to the speculative reformer, to escape that same slight ridicule. Alas for these days of derision and criticism! We call the Beautiful the highest, because it appears to us the golden mean, escaping the dowdiness of the good and the heartlessness of the true. They are lovers of nature also, and find an indemnity in the inviolable order of the world for the violated order and grace of man.

There is, no doubt, a great deal of well-founded objection to be spoken or felt against the sayings and doings of this class, some of whose traits we have selected; no doubt they will lay themselves open to criticism and to lampoons, and as ridiculous stories will be to be told of them as of any. There will be cant and pretension; there will be subtilty and moonshine. These persons are of unequal strength, and do not all prosper. They complain that everything around them must be denied; and if feeble, it takes all their strength to deny, before they can begin to lead their own life. Grave seniors insist on their respect to this institution and that usage; to an obsolete history; to some vocation, or college, or etiquette, or beneficiary, or charity, or morning or evening call, which they resist as what does not concern them. But it costs such sleepless nights, alienations and misgivings, — they have so many moods about it; these old guardians never change *their* minds ; they have but one mood on the subject, namely, that Antony is very perverse, — that it is quite as much as Antony can do to assert his rights, abstain from what he thinks foolish, and keep his temper. He cannot help the reaction of this injustice in his own mind. He is braced-up and stilted ; all freedom and flowing genius, all sallies of wit and frolic nature are quite out of the question ; it is well if he can keep from lying, injustice, and suicide. This is no time for gaiety and grace. His strength and spirits are wasted in rejection. But the strong spirits overpower those around them without effort. Their thought and emotion comes in like a flood, quite withdraws them from all notice of these carping critics ; they surrender themselves with glad heart to the heavenly guide, and only by implication reject the clamorous nonsense of the hour. Grave seniors talk to the deaf, — church and old book mumble and ritualize to an unheeding, preoccupied and advancing mind, and thus they by happiness of greater momentum lose no time, but take the right road at first.

But all these of whom I speak are not profi-
cients; they are novices; they only show the road
in which man should travel, when the soul has
greater health and prowess. Yet let them feel the
dignity of their charge, and deserve a larger power.
Their heart is the ark in which the fire is concealed
which shall burn in a broader and universal flame.
Let them obey the Genius then most when his impulse is wildest; then most when he seems to lead
to uninhabitable deserts of thought and life; for
the path which the hero travels alone is the highway of health and benefit to mankind. What is
the privilege and nobility of our nature but its per-
sistency, through its power to attach itself to what
is permanent?

Society also has its duties in reference to this
class, and must behold them with what charity it
can. Possibly some benefit may yet accrue from
them to the state. In our Mechanics' Fair, there
must be not only bridges, ploughs, carpenters'
planes, and baking troughs, but also some few finer
instruments, — rain gauges, thermometers, and tel-
escopes; and in society, besides farmers, sailors,
and weavers, there must be a few persons of purer
fire kept specially as gauges and meters of character; persons of a fine, detecting instinct, who note
the smallest accumulations of wit and feeling in
the bystander. Perhaps too there might be room

for the exciters and monitors; collectors of the
heavenly spark, with power to convey the electricity to others. Or, as the stormed-tossed vessel at
sea speaks the frigate or ' line packet ' to learn its
longitude, so it may not be without its advantage
that we should now and then encounter rare and
gifted men, to compare the points of our spiritual
compass, and verify our bearings from superior
chronometers.

Amidst the downward tendency and proneness
of things, when every voice is raised for a new
road or another statute or a subscription of stock;
for an improvement in dress, or in dentistry; for
a new house or a larger business; for a political
party, or the division of an estate; — will you not
tolerate one or two solitary voices in the land,
speaking for thoughts and principles not market-
able or perishable? Soon these improvements and
mechanical inventions will be superseded; these
modes of living lost out of memory; these cities
rotted, ruined by war, by new inventions, by new
seats of trade, or the geologic changes: — all gone,
like the shells which sprinkle the sea-beach with
a white colony to-day, forever renewed to be forever destroyed. But the thoughts which these few
hermits strove to proclaim by silence as well as by
speech, not only by what they did, but by what
they forebore to do, shall abide in beauty and

strength, to reorganize themselves in nature, to invest themselves anew in other, perhaps higher endowed and happier mixed clay than ours, in fuller union with the surrounding system.

THE YOUNG AMERICAN.

A LECTURE READ BEFORE THE MERCANTILE LIBRARY ASSO-
CIATION, BOSTON, FEBRUARY 7, 1844.

THE YOUNG AMERICAN.

GENTLEMEN :

IT is remarkable that our people have their intellectual culture from one country and their duties
from another. This false state of things is newly in
a way to be corrected. America is beginning to assert herself to the senses and to the imagination of
her children, and Europe is receding in the same
degree. This their reaction on education gives a
new importance to the internal improvements and
to the politics of the country. Who has not been
stimulated to reflection by the facilities now in progress of construction for travel and the transporta-
tion of goods in the United States?

This rage of road building is beneficent for
America, where vast distance is so main a consideration in our domestic politics and trade, inasmuch as the great political promise of the invention is to hold the Union staunch, whose days
seemed already numbered by the mere inconvenience of transporting representatives, judges, and
officers across such tedious distances of land and

water.   Not only is distance annihilated, but when, as now, the locomotive and the steamboat, like enormous shuttles, shoot every day across the thousand various threads of national descent and employment and bind them fast in one web, an hourly assimilation goes forward, and there is no danger that local peculiarities and hostilities should be preserved.

1. But I hasten to speak of the utility of these improvements in creating an American sentiment. An unlooked for consequence of the railroad is the increased acquaintance it has given the American people with the boundless resources of their own soil.   If this invention has reduced England to a third of its size, by bringing people so much nearer, in this country it has given a new celerity to *time*, or anticipated by fifty years the planting of tracts of land, the choice of water privileges, the working of mines, and other natural advantages.   Railroad iron is a magician's rod, in its power to evoke the sleeping energies of land and water.

The railroad is but one arrow in our quiver, though it has great value as a sort of yard-stick and surveyor's line.   The bountiful continent is ours, state on state, and territory on territory, to the waves of the Pacific sea;

> " Our garden is the immeasurable earth,
> The heaven's blue pillars are Medea's house."

The task of surveying, planting, and building upon this immense tract requires an education and a sentiment commensurate thereto. A consciousness of this fact is beginning to take the place of the purely trading spirit and education which sprang up whilst all the population lived on the fringe of sea-coast. And even on the coast, prudent men have begun to see that every American should be educated with a view to the values of land. The arts of engineering and of architecture are studied; scientific agriculture is an object of growing attention; the mineral riches are explored; limestone, coal, slate, and iron; and the value of timber-lands is enhanced.

Columbus alleged as a reason for seeking a continent in the West, that the harmony of nature required a great tract of land in the western hemisphere, to balance the known extent of land in the eastern; and it now appears that we must estimate the native values of this broad region to redress the balance of our own judgments, and appreciate the advantages opened to the human race in this country which is our fortunate home. The land is the appointed remedy for whatever is false and fantastic in our culture. The continent we inhabit is to be physic and food for our mind, as well as our body. The land, with its tranquilizing, sanative influences, is to repair the errors of a scholastic and

traditional education, and bring us into just relations with men and things.

The habit of living in the presence of these in-
vitations of natural wealth is not inoperative ; and
this habit, combined with the moral sentiment
which, in the recent years, has interrogated every
institution, usage, and law, has naturally given a
strong direction to the wishes and aims of active
young men, to withdraw from cities and cultivate
the soil. This inclination has appeared in the most
unlooked for quarters, in men supposed to be absorbed in business, and in those connected with the
liberal professions. And since the walks of trade
were crowded, whilst that of agriculture cannot
easily be, inasmuch as the farmer who is not wanted
by others can yet grow his own bread, whilst the
manufacturer or the trader, who is not wanted, cannot, — this seemed a happy tendency. For beside
all the moral benefit which we may expect from the
farmer's profession, when a man enters it consid-
erately ; this promised the conquering of the soil,
plenty, and beyond this the adorning of the country
with every advantage and ornament which labor,
ingenuity, and affection for a man's home, could
suggest.

Meantime, with cheap land, and the pacific disposition of the people, everything invites to the arts
of agriculture, of gardening, and domestic archi-

tecture. Public gardens, on the scale of such plantations in Europe and Asia, are now unknown to us. There is no feature of the old countries that strikes an American with more agreeable surprise than the beautiful gardens of Europe ; such as the Boboli in Florence, the Villa Borghese in Rome, the Villa d'Este in Tivoli, the gardens at Munich and at Frankfort on the Main : works easily imitated here, and which might well make the land dear to the citizen, and inflame patriotism. It is the fine art which is left for us, now that sculpture, painting, and religious and civil architecture have become effete, and have passed into second childhood. We have twenty degrees of latitude wherein to choose a seat, and the new modes of travelling enlarge the opportunity of selection, by making it easy to cultivate very distant tracts and yet remain in strict intercourse with the centres of trade and population. And the whole force of all the arts goes to facilitate the decoration of lands and dwellings. A garden has this advantage, that it makes it indifferent where you live. A well-laid garden makes the face of the country of no account ; let that be low or high, grand or mean, you have made a beautiful abode worthy of man. If the landscape is pleasing, the garden shows it, — if tame, it excludes it. A little grove, which any farmer can find or cause to grow near his house, will in a

few years make cataracts and chains of mountains
quite unnecessary to his scenery; and he is so contented with his alleys, woodlands, orchards and
river, that Niagara, and the Notch of the White
Hills, and Nantasket Beach, are superfluities. And
yet the selection of a fit houselot has the same
advantage over an indifferent one, as the selection
to a given employment of a man who has a genius
for that work. In the last case the culture of
years will never make the most painstaking ap-
prentice his equal: no more will gardening give
the advantage of a happy site to a house in a hole
or on a pinnacle. In America we have hitherto
little to boast in this kind. The cities drain the
country of the best part of its population: the
flower of the youth, of both sexes, goes into the
towns, and the country is cultivated by a so much
inferior class. The land, — travel a whole day together, — looks poverty-stricken, and the buildings
plain and poor. In Europe, where society has an
aristocratic structure, the land is full of men of the
best stock and the best culture, whose interest and
pride it is to remain half the year on their estates,
and to fill them with every convenience and ornament. Of course these make model farms, and
model architecture, and are a constant education to
the eye of the surrounding population. Whatever
events in progress shall go to disgust men with

cities and infuse into them the passion for country
life and country pleasures, will render a service to
the whole face of this continent, and will further
the most poetic of all the occupations of real life,
the bringing out by art the native but hidden
graces of the landscape.

I look on such improvements also as directly
tending to endear the land to the inhabitant. Any
relation to the land, the habit of tilling it, or mining it, or even hunting on it, generates the feeling
of patriotism. He who keeps shop on it, or he who
merely uses it as a support to his desk and ledger,
or to his manufactory, values it less. The vast
majority of the people of this country live by the
land, and carry its quality in their manners and
opinions. We in the Atlantic states, by position,
have been commercial, and have, as I said, imbibed
easily an European culture. Luckily for us, now
that steam has narrowed the Atlantic to a strait,
the nervous, rocky West is intruding a new and
continental element into the national mind, and we
shall yet have an American genius. How much
better when the whole land is a garden, and the
people have grown up in the bowers of a paradise.
Without looking then to those extraordinary social
influences which are now acting in precisely this
direction, but only at what is inevitably doing
around us, I think we must regard the *land* as a

commanding and increasing power on the citizen, the sanative and Americanizing influence, which promises to disclose new virtues for ages to come.

2. In the second place, the uprise and culmination of the new and anti-feudal power of Commerce is the political fact of most significance to the American at this hour.

We cannot look on the freedom of this country, in connexion with its youth, without a presentiment that here shall laws and institutions exist on some scale of proportion to the majesty of nature. To men legislating for the area betwixt the two oceans, betwixt the snows and the tropics, somewhat of the gravity of nature will infuse itself into the code. A heterogeneous population crowding on all ships from all corners of the world to the great gates of North America, namely Boston, New York, and New Orleans, and thence proceeding inward to the prairie and the mountains, and quickly contributing their private thought to the public opinion, their toll to the treasury, and their vote to the election, it cannot be doubted that the legislation of this country should become more catholic and cosmopolitan than that of any other. It seems so easy for America to inspire and express the most expansive and humane spirit; new-born, free, healthful, strong, the land of the laborer, of the democrat, of the philanthropist, of the believer, of the saint.

she should speak for the human race. It is the country of the Future. From Washington, proverbially 'the city of magnificent distances,' through all its cities, states, and territories, it is a country of beginnings, of projects, of designs, of expectations.

Gentlemen, there is a sublime and friendly Destiny by which the human race is guided, — the race never dying, the individual never spared, — to results affecting masses and ages. Men are narrow and selfish, but the Genius or Destiny is not narrow, but beneficent. It is not discovered in their calculated and voluntary activity, but in what befalls, with or without their design. Only what is inevitable interests us, and it turns out that love and good are inevitable, and in the course of things. That Genius has infused itself into nature. It indicates itself by a small excess of good, a small balance in brute facts always favorable to the side of reason. All the facts in any part of nature shall be tabulated and the results shall indicate the same security and benefit; so slight as to be hardly observable, and yet it is there. The sphere is flattened at the poles and swelled at the equator; a form flowing necessarily from the fluid state, yet *the* form, the mathematician assures us, required to prevent the protuberances of the continent, or even of lesser mountains cast up at any

time by earthquakes, from continually deranging
the axis of the earth. The census of the population is found to keep an invariable equality in the
sexes, with a trifling predominance in favor of the
male, as if to counterbalance the necessarily increased exposure of male life in war, navigation,
and other accidents. Remark the unceasing effort
throughout nature at somewhat better than the actual creatures: *amelioration in nature*, which alone
permits and authorizes amelioration in mankind.
The population of the world is a conditional population; these are not the best, but the best that
could live in the existing state of soils, gases, animals and morals: the best that could *yet* live;
there shall be a better, please God. This Genius
or Destiny is of the sternest administration, though
rumors exist of its secret tenderness. It may be
styled a cruel kindness, serving the whole even to
the ruin of the member; a terrible communist, re-
serving all profits to the community, without dividend to individuals. Its law is, you shall have
everything as a member, nothing to yourself. For
Nature is the noblest engineer, yet uses a grinding
economy, working up all that is wasted to-day into
to-morrow's creation; — not a superfluous grain of
sand, for all the ostentation she makes of expense
and public works. It is because Nature thus saves
and uses, laboring for the general, that we poor

particulars are so crushed and straitened, and find it so hard to live. She flung us out in her plenty, but we cannot shed a hair or a paring of a nail but instantly she snatches at the shred and appropriates it to the general stock. Our condition is like that of the poor wolves : if one of the flock wound himself or so much as limp, the rest eat him up incontinently.

That serene Power interposes the check upon the caprices and officiousness of our wills. Its charity is not our charity. One of its agents is our will, but that which expresses itself in our will is stronger than our will. We are very forward to help it, but it will not be accelerated. It resists our meddling, eleemosynary contrivances. We devise sumptuary and relief laws, but the principle of population is always reducing wages to the lowest pittance on which human life can be sustained. We legislate against forestalling and monopoly ; we would have a common granary for the poor ; but the selfishness which hoards the corn for high prices is the preventive of famine ; and the law of self-preservation is surer policy than any legislation can be. We concoct eleemosynary systems, and it turns out that our charity increases pauperism. We inflate our paper currency, we repair commerce with unlimited credit, and are presently visited with unlimited bankruptcy.

It is easy to see that the existing generation are conspiring with a beneficence which in its working for coming generations, sacrifices the passing one ; which infatuates the most selfish men to act against their private interest for the public welfare. We build railroads, we know not for what or for whom ; but one thing is certain, that we who build will receive the very smallest share of benefit. Benefit will accrue, they are essential to the country, but that will be felt not until we are no longer countrymen. We do the like in all matters : —

> " Man's heart the Almighty to the Future set
> By secret and inviolable springs."

We plant trees, we build stone houses, we redeem the waste, we make prospective laws, we found colleges and hospitals, for remote generations. We should be mortified to learn that the little benefit we chanced in our own persons to receive was the utmost they would yield.

The history of commerce is the record of this beneficent tendency. The patriarchal form of government readily becomes despotic, as each person may see in his own family. Fathers wish to be fathers of the minds of their children, and behold with impatience a new character and way of thinking presuming to show itself in their own son or daughter. This feeling, which all their love and pride in the powers of their children cannot subdue, becomes petulance and tyranny when the head of the clan, the emperor of an empire, deals with the same difference of opinion in his subjects. Difference of opinion is the one crime which kings never forgive. An empire is an immense egotism. "I am the State," said the French Louis. When a French ambassador mentioned to Paul of Russia that a man of consequence in St. Petersburg was interesting himself in some matter, the Czar interrupted him, — "There is no man of consequence in this empire but he with whom I am actually speaking; and so long only as I am speaking to him is he of any consequence." And the Emperor Nicholas is reported to have said to his council, "The age is embarrassed with new opinions; rely on me gentlemen, I shall oppose an iron will to the progress of liberal opinions."

It is easy to see that this patriarchal or family management gets to be rather troublesome to all but the papa; the sceptre comes to be a crow-bar. And this unpleasant egotism, Feudalism opposes and finally destroys. The king is compelled to call in the aid of his brothers and cousins and remote relations, to help him keep his overgrown house in order; and this club of noblemen always come at last to have a will of their own; they combine to brave the sovereign, and call in the aid of the people. Each chief attaches as many followers as he can, by kindness, maintenance, and gifts ; and as long as war lasts, the nobles, who must be soldiers, rule very well. But when peace comes, the nobles prove very whimsical and uncomfortable masters ; their frolics turn out to be insulting and degrading to the commoner. Feudalism grew to be a bandit and brigand.

Meantime Trade had begun to appear : Trade, a plant which grows wherever there is peace, as soon as there is peace, and as long as there is peace. The luxury and necessity of the noble fostered it. And as quickly as men go to foreign parts in ships or caravans, a new order of things springs up ; new command takes place, new servants and new masters. Their information, their wealth, their correspondence, have made them quite other men than left their native shore. *They* are nobles now, and by another patent than the king's. Feudalism had been good, had broken the power of the kings, and had some good traits of its own ; but it had grown mischievous, it was time for it to die, and as they say of dying people, all its faults came out. Trade was the strong man that broke it down and raised a new and unknown power in its place. It is a new agent in the world, and one of great function ; it is a very intellectual force. This displaces physical strength and instals computation, combination, information, science, in its room. It calls out all force of a certain kind that slumbered in the former dynasties. It is now in the midst of its career. Feudalism is not ended yet. Our governments still partake largely of that element. Trade goes to make the governments insignificant, and to bring every kind of faculty of every individual that can in any manner serve any person, *on sale.* Instead of a huge Army and Navy and Executive Departments, it converts Government into an Intelligence-Office, where every man may find what he wishes to buy, and expose what he has to sell; not only produce and manufactures, but art, skill, and intellectual and moral values. This is the good and this the evil of trade, that it would put everything into market; talent, beauty, virtue, and man himself.

The philosopher and lover of man have much harm to say of trade; but the historian will see that trade was the principle of Liberty; that trade planted America and destroyed Feudalism; that it makes peace and keeps peace, and it will abolish slavery. We complain of its oppression of the poor, and of its building up a new aristocracy on the ruins of the aristocracy it destroyed. But the aristocracy of trade has no permanence, is not entailed, was the result of toil and talent, the result of merit of some kind, and is continually falling, like the waves of the sea, before new claims of the same sort. Trade is an instrument in the hands of that friendly Power which works for us in our own despite. We design it thus and thus; it turns out otherwise and far better. This beneficent tendency, omnipotent without violence, exists and works. Every line of history inspires a confidence that we shall not go far wrong ; that things mend. That is the moral of all we learn, that it warrants Hope, the prolific mother of reforms. Our part is plainly not to throw ourselves across the track, to block improvement and sit till we are stone, but to watch the uprise of successive mornings and to conspire with the new works of new days. Government has been a fossil ; it should be a plant. I conceive that the office of statute law should be to express and not to impede the mind of mankind. New thoughts, new things. Trade was one instrument, but Trade is also but for a time, and must give way to somewhat broader and better, whose signs are already dawning in the sky.

3. I pass to speak of the signs of that which is the sequel of trade.

In consequence of the revolution in the state of society wrought by trade, Government in our times is beginning to wear a clumsy and cumbrous appearance. We have already seen our way to shorter methods. The time is full of good signs. Some of them shall ripen to fruit. All this bene-

ficent socialism is a friendly omen, and the swelling
cry of voices for the education of the people indicates that Government has other offices than those
of banker and executioner. Witness the new movements in the civilized world, the Communism of
France, Germany, and Switzerland; the Trades'
Unions, the English League against the Corn Laws;
and the whole *Industrial Statistics*, so called. In
Paris, the blouse, the badge of the operative, has
begun to make its appearance in the saloons. Witness too the spectacle of three Communities which
have within a very short time sprung up within
this Commonwealth, besides several others under-
taken by citizens of Massachusetts within the territory of other States. These proceeded from a
variety of motives, from an impatience of many
usages in common life, from a wish for greater freedom than the manners and opinions of society permitted, but in great part from a feeling that the
true offices of the State, the State had let fall to the
ground; that in the scramble of parties for the
public purse, the main duties of government were
omitted, — the duty to instruct the ignorant, to
supply the poor with work and with good guidance.
These communists preferred the agricultural life as
the most favorable condition for human culture;
but they thought that the farm, as we manage it,
did not satisfy the right ambition of man. The

farmer, after sacrificing pleasure, taste, freedom, thought, love, to his work, turns out often a bankrupt, like the merchant. This result might well seem astounding. All this drudgery, from cock-crowing to starlight, for all these years, to end in mortgages and the auctioneer's flag, and removing from bad to worse. It is time to have the thing looked into, and with a sifting criticism ascertained who is the fool. It seemed a great deal worse, because the farmer is living in the same town with men who pretend to know exactly what he wants. On one side is agricultural chemistry, coolly exposing the nonsense of our spendthrift agriculture and ruinous expense of manures, and offering, by means of a teaspoonful of artificial guano, to turn a sandbank into corn; and on the other, the farmer, not only eager for the information, but with bad crops and in debt and bankruptcy, for want of it. Here are Etzlers and mechanical projectors, who, with the Fourierists, undoubtingly affirm that the smallest union would make every man rich; — and, on the other side, a multitude of poor men and women seeking work, and who cannot find enough to pay their board. The science is confident, and surely the poverty is real. If any means could be found to bring these two together !

This was one design of the projectors of the Associations which are now making their first feeble experiments. They were founded in love and in labor. They proposed, as you know, that all men should take a part in the manual toil, and proposed to amend the condition of men by substituting harmonious for hostile industry. It was a noble thought of Fourier, which gives a favorable idea of his system, to distinguish in his Phalanx a class as the Sacred Band, by whom whatever duties were disagreeable and likely to be omitted, were to be assumed.

At least an economical success seemed certain for the enterprise, and that agricultural association must, sooner or later, fix the price of bread, and drive single farmers into association in self-defence; as the great commercial and manufacturing companies had already done. The Community is only the continuation of the same movement which made the joint-stock companies for manufactures, mining, insurance, banking, and so forth. It has turned out cheaper to make calico by companies; and it is proposed to plant corn and to bake bread by companies.

Undoubtedly, abundant mistakes will be made by these first adventurers, which will draw ridicule on their schemes. I think for example that they exaggerate the importance of a favorite project of theirs, that of paying talent and labor at one rate, paying all sorts of service at one rate, say ten cents the hour. They have paid it so; but not an instant would a dime remain a dime. In one hand it became an eagle as it fell, and in another hand a copper cent. For the whole value of the dime is in knowing what to do with it. One man buys with it a land-title of an Indian, and makes his posterity princes; or buys corn enough to feed the world; or pen, ink, and paper, or a painter's brush, by which he can communicate himself to the human race as if he were fire; and the other buys barley candy. Money is of no value; it cannot spend itself. All depends on the skill of the spender. Whether too the objection almost universally felt by such women in the community as were mothers, to an associate life, to a common table, and a common nursery, etc., setting a higher value on the private family, with poverty, than on an association with wealth, will not prove insuperable, remains to be determined.

But the Communities aimed at a higher success in securing to all their members an equal and thorough education. And on the whole one may say that aims so generous and so forced on them by the times, will not be relinquished, even if these attempts fail, but will be prosecuted until they succeed.

This is the value of the Communities; not what they have done, but the revolution which they indicate as on the way. Yes, Government must edu-

THE YOUNG AMERICAN.

cate the poor man. Look across the country from any hill-side around us and the landscape seems to crave Government. The actual differences of men must be acknowledged, and met with love and wisdom. These rising grounds which command the champaign below, seem to ask for lords, true lords, *land*-lords, who understand the land and its uses and the applicabilities of men, and whose government would be what it should, namely mediation between want and supply. How gladly would each citizen pay a commission for the support and continuation of good guidance. None should be a governor who has not a talent for governing. Now many people have a native skill for carving out business for many hands; a genius for the disposition of affairs; and are never happier than when difficult practical questions, which embarrass other men, are to be solved. All lies in light before them; they are in their element. Could any means be contrived to appoint only these! There really seems a progress towards such a state of things in which this work shall be done by these natural workmen; and this, not certainly through any increased discretion shown by the citizens at elections, but by the gradual contempt into which official government falls, and the increasing disposition of private adventurers to assume its fallen functions. Thus the national Post

Office is likely to go into disuse before the private telegraph and the express companies. The currency threatens to fall entirely into private hands. Justice is continually administered more and more by private reference, and not by litigation. We have feudal governments in a commercial age. It would be but an easy extension of our commercial system, to pay a private emperor a fee for services, as we pay an architect, an engineer, or a lawyer. If any man has a talent for righting wrong, for administering difficult affairs, for counselling poor farmers how to turn their estates to good husbandry, for combining a hundred private enterprises to a general benefit, let him in the county-town, or in Court Street, put up his sign-board, Mr. Smith, *Governor*, Mr. Johnson, *Working king*.

How can our young men complain of the poverty of things in New England, and not feel that poverty as a demand on their charity to make New England rich ? Where is he who seeing a thousand men useless and unhappy, and making the whole region forlorn by their inaction, and conscious himself of possessing the faculty they want, does not hear his call to go and be their king ?

We must have kings, and we must have nobles. Nature provides such in every society, — only let us have the real instead of the titular. Let us have our leading and our inspiration from the best.

In every society some men are born to rule and some to advise. Let the powers be well directed, directed by love, and they would everywhere be greeted with joy and honor. The chief is the chief all the world over, only not his cap and his plume. It is only their dislike of the pretender, which makes men sometimes unjust to the accomplished man. If society were transparent, the noble would everywhere be gladly received and accredited, and would not be asked for his day's work, but would be felt as benefit, inasmuch as he was noble. That were his duty and stint, — to keep himself pure and purifying, the leaven of his nation. I think I see place and duties for a nobleman in every society; but it is not to drink wine and ride in a fine coach, but to guide and adorn life for the multitude by forethought, by elegant studies, by perseverance, self-devotion, and the remembrance of the humble old friend, by making his life secretly beautiful.

I call upon you, young men, to obey your heart and be the nobility of this land. In every age of the world there has been a leading nation, one of a more generous sentiment, whose eminent citizens were willing to stand for the interests of general justice and humanity, at the risk of being called, by the men of the moment, chimerical and fantastic. Which should be that nation but these States?

Which should lead that movement, if not New England? Who should lead the leaders, but the Young American? The people, and the world, are now suffering from the want of religion and honor in its public mind. In America, out-of-doors all seems a market; in-doors an air-tight stove of conventionalism. Every body who comes into our houses savors of these habits; the men, of the market; the women, of the custom. I find no expression in our state papers or legislative debate, in our lyceums or churches, especially in our newspapers, of a high national feeling, no lofty counsels that rightfully stir the blood. I speak of those organs which can be presumed to speak a popular sense. They recommend conventional virtues, whatever will earn and preserve property; always the capitalist; the college, the church, the hospital, the theatre, the hotel, the road, the ship of the capitalist, — whatever goes to secure, adorn, enlarge these is good; what jeopardizes any of these is damnable. The 'opposition' papers, so called, are on the same side. They attack the great capitalist, but with the aim to make a capitalist of the poor man. The opposition is against those who have money, from those who wish to have money. But who announces to us in journal, or in pulpit, or in the street, the secret of heroism?

> " Man alone
> Can perform the impossible."

I shall not need to go into an enumeration of our national defects and vices which require this Order of Censors in the State. I might not set down our most proclaimed offences as the worst. It is not often the worst trait that occasions the loudest outcry. Men complain of their suffering, and not of the crime. I fear little from the bad effect of Repudiation; I do not fear that it will spread. Stealing is a suicidal business; you cannot repudiate but once. But the bold face and tardy repentance permitted to this local mischief reveal a public mind so preoccupied with the love of gain that the common sentiment of indignation at fraud does not act with its natural force. The more need of a withdrawal from the crowd, and a resort to the fountain of right, by the brave. The timidity of our public opinion is our disease, or, shall I say, the publicness of opinion, the absence of private opinion. Good nature is plentiful, but we want justice, with heart of steel, to fight down the proud. The private mind has the access to the totality of goodness and truth that it may be a balance to a corrupt society; and to stand for the private verdict against popular clamor is the office of the noble. If a humane measure is propounded in behalf of the slave, or of the Irishman, or the Catholic, or for the succor of the poor; that sentiment, that project, will have the homage of the hero. That is his nobility, his oath of knighthood, to succor the helpless and oppressed ; always to throw himself on the side of weakness, of youth, of hope; on the liberal, on the expansive side, never on the defensive, the conserving, the timorous, the lock-and-bolt system. More than our good-will we may not be able to give. We have our own affairs, our own genius, which chains each to his proper work. We cannot give our life to the cause of the debtor, of the slave, or the pauper, as another is doing; but to one thing we are bound, not to blaspheme the sentiment and the work of that man, not to throw stumbling-blocks in the way of the abolitionist, the philanthropist; as the organs of influence and opinion are swift to do. It is for us to confide in the beneficent Supreme Power, and not to rely on our money, and on the state because it is the guard of money. At this moment, the terror of old people and of vicious people is lest the Union of these states be destroyed : as if the Union had any other real basis than the good pleasure of a majority of the citizens to be united. But the wise and just man will always feel that he stands on his own feet; that he imparts strength to the State, not receives security from it; and that if all went down, he and such as he would quite easily combine in a new and better constitution. Every great and memorable community has consisted of formidable individuals, who, like the Roman or the Spartan, lent his own spirit to the State and made it great. Yet only by the supernatural is a man strong; nothing is so weak as an egotist. Nothing is mightier than we, when we are vehicles of a truth before which the State and the individual are alike ephemeral.

Gentlemen, the development of our American internal resources, the extension to the utmost of the commercial system, and the appearance of new moral causes which are to modify the State, are giving an aspect of greatness to the Future, which the imagination fears to open. One thing is plain for all men of common sense and common conscience, that here, here in America, is the home of man. After all the deductions which are to be made for our pitiful politics, which stake every gravest national question on the silly die whether James or whether Robert shall sit in the chair and hold the purse; after all the deduction is made for our frivolities and insanities, there still remains an organic simplicity and liberty, which, when it loses its balance, redresses itself presently, which offers opportunity to the human mind not known in any other region.

It is true, the public mind wants self-respect. We are full of vanity, of which the most signal proof is our sensitiveness to foreign and especially

English censure. One cause of this is our immense reading, and that reading chiefly confined to the productions of the English press. It is also true that to imaginative persons in this country there is somewhat bare and bald in our short history and unsettled wilderness. They ask, who would live in a new country that can live in an old? and it is not strange that our youths and maidens should burn to see the picturesque extremes of an antiquated country. But it is one thing to visit the Pyramids, and another to wish to live there. Would they like tithes to the clergy, and sevenths to the government, and Horse-Guards, and licensed press, and grief when a child is born, and threatening, starved weavers, and a pauperism now constituting one thirteenth of the population? Instead of the open future expanding here before the eye of every boy to vastness, would they like the closing in of the future to a narrow slit of sky, and that fast contracting to be no future? One thing for instance, the beauties of aristocracy, we commend to the study of the travelling American. The English, the most conservative people this side of India, are not sensible of the restraint, but an American would seriously resent it. The aristocracy, incorporated by law and education, degrades life for the unprivileged classes. It is a questionable compensation to the embittered feeling of a

proud commoner, the reflection that a fop, who, by
the magic of title, paralyzes his arm and plucks
from him half the graces and rights of a man, is
himself also an aspirant excluded with the same
ruthlessness from higher circles, since there is no
end to the wheels within wheels of this spiral heaven. Something may be pardoned to the spirit of
loyalty when it becomes fantastic; and something
to the imagination, for the baldest life is symbolic.
Philip II. of Spain rated his ambassador for neg-
lecting serious affairs in Italy, whilst he debated
some point of honor with the French ambassador ;
" You have left a business of importance for a ceremony." The ambassador replied, " Your Majesty's self is but a ceremony." In the East, where
the religious sentiment comes in to the support of
the aristocracy, and in the Romish church also,
there is a grain of sweetness in the tyranny ; but
in England, the fact seems to me intolerable, what
is commonly affirmed, that such is the transcendent
honor accorded to wealth and birth, that no man
of letters, be his eminence what it may, is received
into the best society, except as a lion and a show.
The English have many virtues, many advantages,
and the proudest history of the world ; but they
need all and more than all the resources of the
past to indemnify a heroic gentleman in that country for the mortifications prepared for him by the

system of society, and which seem to impose the alternative to resist or to avoid it. That there are mitigations and practical alleviations to this rigor, is not an excuse for the rule. Commanding worth and personal power must sit crowned in all companies, nor will extraordinary persons be slighted or affronted in any company of civilized men. But the system is an invasion of the sentiment of justice and the native rights of men, which, however decorated, must lessen the value of English citizenship. It is for Englishmen to consider, not for us; we only say, Let us live in America, too thankful for our want of feudal institutions. Our houses and towns are like mosses and lichens, so slight and new; but youth is a fault of which we shall daily mend. This land too is as old as the Flood, and wants no ornament or privilege which nature could bestow. Here stars, here woods, here hills, here animals, here men abound, and the vast tendencies concur of a new order. If only the men are employed in conspiring with the designs of the Spirit who led us hither and is leading us still, we shall quickly enough advance out of all hearing of others' censures, out of all regrets of our own, into a new and more excellent social state than history has recorded.